beds &
borders

beds & borders

simple projects for
the weekend gardener

Richard Bird

photography by Stephen Robson

RYLAND
PETERS
& SMALL

LONDON NEW YORK

For this edition:

Senior designer *Sally Powell*

Senior editor *Clare Double*

Production *Sheila Smith*

Art director *Gabriella Le Grazie*

Publishing director *Alison Starling*

Illustrators *Martine Collings, Tracy Fennell,
Valerie Hill, Stephen Hird, Sarah Kensington,
Amanda Patton, Elizabeth Pepperell, Lizzie
Sanders, Helen Smythe, Ann Winterbotham*

First published in the USA in 1998.
This new edition published in 2005 by
Ryland Peters & Small, Inc.
519 Broadway, 5th Floor
New York, NY 10012
www.rylandpeters.com

10 9 8 7 6 5 4 3 2 1

Printed and bound in China.

Library of Congress Cataloging-in-Publication Data

Bird, Richard, 1942-
  Beds & borders : simple projects for the weekend
gardener / Richard Bird ; photography by Stephen
Robson.-- New ed.
      p. cm.
  Includes index.
  ISBN 1-84172-925-6 (hardback) -- ISBN 1-84172-
806-3 (pbk.)
  1. Beds (Gardens) 2. Garden borders. 3. Plants,
Ornamental. I. Title: Beds and borders. II. Title.

SB423.7.B556 2005
635.9'62--dc22

                              2004021184

contents

introduction 6

traditional borders 8
perennial border 10
single-color bed 14
carpet bed 18
foliage bed 22
mixed border 26
purple and yellow 30

shaped borders 34
round bed 36
parterre 40
corner planting 44

special borders 48
waterside planting 50
dry border 54
woodland border 58
mediterranean border 62
shady border 66
rose bed 70

walk-through borders 74
edible border 76
cottage garden path 80
scented path 84
raised flower bed 88
rose trellis walk 92

basic techniques 96
useful addresses 102
index 104
credits 110
acknowledgments 112

introduction

The use of borders is the very essence of gardening. They are a means of producing a pleasant environment that is a joy to be in. They can excite or soothe depending on the mood created. They can be filled with color or present a mantle of foliage. Beds and borders can appeal to all the senses: the sense of smell, of course, and sound —why not plant a bed especially to enjoy the soothing rustle of leaves, grasses, and bamboos, easing the mind—and even taste, as many flowers are edible. Borders are the backdrop against which you can relax and enjoy the pleasures of an outside space.

The projects in this book cover a broad range of borders that can be created using a wide variety of plants. Most can be modified for any size garden, from a small courtyard to a number of acres. Adaptability is the key. While you are free to copy faithfully what is described, you are encouraged to experiment and extend your own experience. Add or substitute plants that you like or whose colors you prefer. Use this book as a jumping-off point, and with patience your efforts will be amply rewarded.

Richard Bird

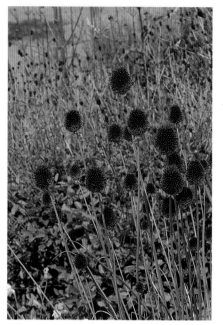

traditional borders

take many forms and can be adapted at will to suit any garden. Annuals bring a flash of strong color or subtler hue and are ideal for graphic planting schemes; single colors bring harmony; and the classic perennial border cannot be matched for the impression of abundance and variety it lends to a garden. Borders and beds are important focal points so they should be created with care.

above left Formality is not always wanted. Here, cottage-style charm is given by *Allium schoenoprasum*, or chives.

above center Mixed borders allow a variety of shapes and forms: pincushion flowers and salvias mingle with roses.

above right Always consider how flower forms will combine as well as colors. A cluster of star shapes looks cheerful.

center right A well-conceived border will give color, height, variety, and a clear mood to a garden. It will add inspiring forefront focus or clear background interest to a view.

right Fill vertical spaces so that the eye is led through the design, as here. Low-growing edging plants are linked by the midheight lilies to a prominent honeysuckle-clad rose. The space is well filled without appearing congested.

above Foliage is there to be enjoyed in its own right as well as to make a fine foil to bold blooms. It affords a wealth of shapes, textures, and colors, as well as the permanence of evergreen displays.

below Plants have a way of softening edges and blending. Fanning phlox, foxgloves, and alliums weave toward dark columbines.

above A harmonious color scheme in a border can be enhanced by using a similar palette beyond the border. Here, mullein is coupled with the soft yellow rose 'Graham Thomas,' and *Rosa* 'Frau Karl Druschki.'

left Movement and rhythm are at the heart of this interesting foliage scheme, which is punctuated by subtle flower tones.

perennial border

Perennial borders are back. Having suffered a decline in the earlier part of the twentieth century, interest in herbaceous plants has never been so great. They are versatile, presenting the gardener with a tremendous range of colors, shapes, textures, and scents, and despite a reputation for being labor-intensive, they take less looking after than many shrubs, such as roses. For those who have been wary of using perennial plants, a whole new world is here to be explored.

PLANTING SCHEME

Achillea millefolium 'Cerise Queen' (x 5)

Achillea filipendulina 'Gold Plate' (x 6)

Alchemilla mollis (x 3)

Aquilegia 'Crimson Star' (x 9)

Asphodeline lutea (x 5)

Astilbe chinensis var. pumila (x 3)

Eremurus subsp. stenophyllus (x 1)

Euphorbia griffithii 'Fireglow' (x 3)

Helenium autumnale (x 3)

Helianthus 'Loddon Gold' (x 1)

Hemerocallis 'Marion Vaughn' (x 1)

Kniphofia 'Percy's Pride' (x 1)

Lychnis chalcedonica (x 3)

Malva moschata (x 3)

Mimulus 'Royal Velvet' (x 3)

Nectaroscordum siculum (x 12)

Oenothera fruticosa 'Fyreverken' (x 2)

Oenothera stricta (x 2)

Penstemon 'Andenken an Friedrich Hahn' (x 1)

Polemonium pauciflorum (x 4)

Sedum 'Ruby Glow' (x 2)

Solidago cutleri (x 1)

Solidago 'Laurin' (x 1)

Trifolium rubens (x 1)

Verbascum bombyciferum (x 3)

planting scheme

1 *Achillea millefolium* 'Cerise Queen'
  (x 5)
2 *Achillea filipendulina* 'Gold Plate' (x 6)
3 *Alchemilla mollis* (x 3)
4 *Aquilegia* 'Crimson Star' (x 9)
5 *Asphodeline lutea* (x 5)
6 *Astilbe chinensis* var. *pumila* (x 3)
7 *Eremurus* subsp. *stenophyllus* (x 1)
8 *Euphorbia griffithii* 'Fireglow' (x 3)
9 *Helenium autumnale* (x 3)
10 *Helianthus* 'Loddon Gold' (x 1)
11 *Hemerocallis* 'Marion Vaughn' (x 1)
12 *Kniphofia* 'Percy's Pride' (x 1)
13 *Lychnis chalcedonica* (x 3)

14 *Malva moschata* (x 3)
15 *Mimulus* 'Royal Velvet' (x 3)
16 *Nectaroscordum siculum* (x 12)
17 *Oenothera fruticosa* 'Fyreverken' (x 2)
18 *Oenothera stricta* (x 2)
19 *Penstemon* 'Andenken an Friedrich
  Hahn' (x 1)
20 *Polemonium pauciflorum* (x 4)
21 *Sedum* 'Ruby Glow' (x 2)
22 *Solidago cutleri* (x 1)
23 *Solidago* 'Laurin' (x 1)
24 *Trifolium rubens* (x 1)
25 *Verbascum bombyciferum* (x 3)

The secret of creating a successful perennial border is to make certain that the ground is prepared thoroughly before planting begins. It is essential that all perennial weeds are removed, and generous quantities of well-rotted organic matter are added, because the border will not be dug again for several years. Such preparations are well worth the time and effort involved.

designing

There is no definitive shape for a perennial border; it should be designed to fit the space available. However, if possible, the bed should be wide; the ideal is a width of at least twice the height of the tallest plants to be used. This border is 12 x 20 ft (3.5 x 6 m). A backdrop of a green hedge will help to display the flowers to advantage, although an island bed makes a fine focal point. The border should have the tallest flowers at the back and shorter ones toward the front. Plan the arrangement of plants on paper before planting and create year-round interest by including plants for each season.

spacing

If you want to create an abundant look quickly, arrange the plants in close proximity. If you can wait, which is better, allow more growing room.

spring underplanting

Perennial borders usually come into their own from early summer onward. Because of the dense growth required to keep a plant in flower right through to autumn, it is difficult to accommodate spring flowers as well. However, there are a few, bulbs in particular, that can be used because they soon die back and take up little or no space later in the year. Cool-season pansies and forget-me-nots can be taken out as the herbaceous growth begins.

alternative planting

1 *Delphinium* hybrids (x 6)
2 *Campanula portenschlagiana* (x 3)
3 *Veronica* 'Shirley Blue' (x 3)
4 *Veronica longifolia* (x 3)
5 *Eryngium alpinum* (x 3)
6 *Geranium* 'Johnson's Blue' (x 1)
7 *Salvia uliginosa* (x 3)
8 *Salvia × sylvestris* 'Blauhügel' (x 1)
9 *Aster × frikartii* 'Mönch' (x 1)
10 *Agapanthus* 'Bressingham Blue' (x 3)
11 *Echinops ritro* (x 1)
12 *Perovskia atriplicifolia* (x 1)
13 *Campanula lactiflora* (x 1)
14 *Aster ericoides* 'Blue Star' (x 1)
15 *Miscanthus sinensis* (x 1)
16 *Salvia sclarea* var. *turkestanica* (x 3)
17 *Bupleurum falcatum* (x 3)
18 *Argyranthemum* 'Jamaica Primrose' (x 3)
19 *Antirrhinum* 'Yellow Triumph' (x 5)
20 *Lilium* 'Limelight' (x 3)
21 *Kniphofia* 'Yellow Hammer' (x 1)
22 *Oenothera stricta* (x 3)
23 *Verbascum bombyciferum* (x 5)
24 *Baptisia australis* (x 1)
25 *Nigella damascena* (x 5)

selecting colors

Since perennials are so diverse, the palette of a bed can be controlled very successfully. This alternative layout is "cool" where the main design is "hot."

care and maintenance

- In autumn, tidy the border, removing dead and dying growth; follow with a mulch.
- Make sure the bed does not become too congested, because this can harm and even kill plants.
- Divide vigorous plants regularly, discarding the older sections.

13

single-color bed

Nothing impresses visitors to a garden as much as a border devoted to one color. The white garden at Sissinghurst and the red one at Hidcote, two of the finest English gardens, are famous throughout the world and have been much copied. Even when inspiration is taken from an exemplary planting, individual gardeners can make their own choice and arrangement of plants, creating a single-color border very much their own.

PLANTING SCHEME

perennials

Alcea rugosa (x 3)

Anemone hupehensis var. *japonica* 'Prinz Heinrich' (x 3)

Aster novi-belgii 'Carnival' (x 3)

Aster novae-angliae 'Andenken an Alma Pötschke' (x 3)

Astilbe × arendsii 'Fanal' (x 3)

Centranthus ruber (x 3)

Echinacea purpurea (x 3)

Filipendula rubra (x 5)

Geranium psilostemon (x 1)

Geranium 'Ann Folkard' (x 1)

Lupinus 'The Chatelaine' (x 1)

Lychnis viscaria 'Flore Pleno' (x 3)

Lythrum virgatum 'The Rocket' (x 2)

Penstemon 'Evelyn' (x 1)

Penstemon 'Andenken an Friedrich Hahn' (x 1)

Persicaria affinis (x 3)

Physostegia virginiana 'Red Beauty' (x 3)

Sanguisorba obtusa (x 3)

Sedum telephium subsp. *maximum* 'Atropurpureum' (x 3)

Sedum spectabile (x 3)

bulbs

Crinum × powellii (x 3)

Dahlia 'Betty Bowen' (x 3)

Schizostylis coccinea (x 5)

Tulipa 'Queen of Night' (x 7)

shrubs

Deutzia × elegantissima (x 1)

Rosa 'Mme Isaac Pereire' (x 1)

annuals

Antirrhinum majus 'His Excellency' (x 7)

Atriplex hortensis var. *rubra* (x 5)

Dianthus chinensis 'Firecarpet' (x 5)

Papaver somniferum (x 3)

Verbena 'Showtime' (x 7)

planting scheme

perennials

1 *Alcea rugosa* (x 3)

2 *Anemone hupehensis* var. *japonica* 'Prinz Heinrich' (x 3)

3 *Aster novi-belgii* 'Carnival' (x 3)

4 *Aster novae-angliae* 'Andenken an Alma Pötschke' (x 3)

5 *Astilbe × arendsii* 'Fanal' (x 3)

6 *Centranthus ruber* (x 3)

7 *Echinacea purpurea* (x 3)

8 *Filipendula rubra* (x 5)

9 *Geranium psilostemon* (x 1)

10 *Geranium* 'Ann Folkard' (x 1)

11 *Lupinus* 'The Chatelaine' (x 1)

12 *Lychnis viscaria* 'Flore Pleno' (x 3)

13 *Lythrum virgatum* 'The Rocket' (x 2)

14 *Penstemon* 'Evelyn' (x 1)

15 *Penstemon* 'Andenken an Friedrich Hahn' (x 1)

16 *Persicaria affinis* (x 3)

17 *Physostegia virginiana* 'Red Beauty' (x 3)

18 *Sanguisorba obtusa* (x 3)

19 *Sedum telephium* subsp. *maximum* 'Atropurpureum' (x 3)

20 *Sedum spectabile* (x 3)

bulbs

21 *Crinum × powellii* (x 3)

22 *Dahlia* 'Betty Bowen' (x 3)

23 *Schizostylis coccinea* (x 5)

24 *Tulipa* 'Queen of Night' (x 7)

shrubs

25 *Deutzia × elegantissima* (x 1)

26 *Rosa* 'Mme Isaac Pereire' (x 1)

annuals

27 *Antirrhinum majus* 'His Excellency' (x 7)

28 *Atriplex hortensis* var. *rubra* (x 5)

29 *Dianthus chinensis* 'Firecarpet' (x 5)

30 *Papaver somniferum* (x 3)

31 *Verbena* 'Showtime' (x 7)

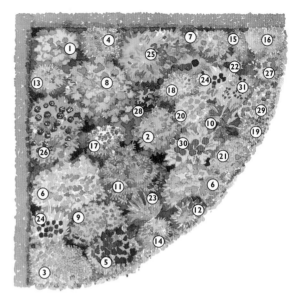

secondary colors

Introducing a second color into what is predominantly a single-colored border can be most effective. The second color might serve to create a focal point or to relieve what has become a dull scene. The overall color scheme is retained but made more interesting.

Although it may seem a simple goal, creating a border from a single color is not easy. There are many different shades of any one color and they do not always combine well. Yellow, for example, has two distinct forms, orange-yellows and green-yellows. Similarly, blue-reds and orange-reds are quite different in character and do not mix. There are no fixed rules for evaluating a plant's color and it is really a question of developing an eye for blending tones.

the foliage factor

Most green leaves complement a wide range of flower colors. Variegated plants, however, should be used with caution: a strident golden variegation in the middle of this romantic pink corner bed, 12 x 12 ft (3.5 x 3.5 m), would spoil the effect completely. Similarly, silver and purple foliage can strike a jarring note unless they take up the theme of your color scheme, so always look beyond the shade of the flower to the foliage effect to avoid disappointment. To be true to your scheme, remove any mismatched plants.

alternative scheme: a white border

The classic single-color border is white, which produces a timeless, restful effect. Pure whites and creamy whites do not combine well, so select plants with care.

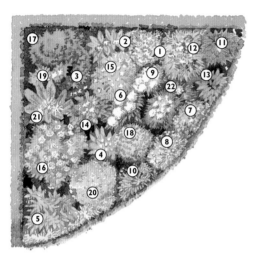

alternative planting

perennials

1 *Achillea ptarmica* The Pearl Group (x 3)
2 *Digitalis purpurea* 'Alba' (x 3)
3 *Anemone × hybrida* 'Honorine Jobert' (x 3)
4 *Gypsophila paniculata* 'Bristol Fairy' (x 1)
5 *Polygonatum × hybridum* (x 1)
6 *Phlox paniculata* 'Fujiyama' (x 1)
7 *Lamium maculatum* 'White Nancy' (x 3)
8 *Dianthus* 'Haytor White' (x 3)
9 *Anaphalis margaritacea* (x 1)
10 *Stachys byzantina* (x 3)
11 *Smilacina racemosa* (x 1)
12 *Epilobium angustifolium* 'Album' (x 2)
13 *Pulmonaria officinalis* 'Sissinghurst White' (x 3)

bulbs

14 *Tulipa* 'Maureen' (x 6)
15 *Cosmos* 'Purity' (x 4)

shrubs

16 *Rosa* 'Iceberg' (x 1)
17 *Exochorda × macrantha* 'The Bride' (x 1)
18 *Artemisia* 'Powis Castle' (x 1)
19 *Clematis* 'Marie Boisselot' (x 1)

annuals

20 *Omphalodes linifolia* (x 5)
21 *Nicotiana sylvestris* (x 3)
22 *Antirrhinum* 'White Wonder' (x 5)

seasonal interest

The essential factor to remember for all borders is seasonal interest. A border or bed is not truly successful if its period of interest is limited to a glorious midsummer display, with nothing of significance in spring, late summer, or fall. With single-color beds the challenge is all the greater to find early- and late-flowering plants that take up the color idea. This consistency is important because seasons of interest overlap.

carpet bed

Among the most colorful elements of Victorian gardens were carpet beds. Some designs were simple, just blocks of colors, while others were complicated patterns that involved thousands of plants. By using a cold frame or greenhouse it is possible to produce all the plants required for a bedding display at low cost, and the rewards are great for the effort needed. Especially effective as front gardens, these borders will make their mark in any formal design.

PLANTING SCHEME

Cordyline australis (x 1)

Echeveria pulvinata (x 8 per yd/per m)

Echeveria secunda var. *glauca* (x 8 per yd/per m)

Sedum acre (x 150 per sq yd/per sq m)

Echeveria elegans (x 10 per yd/per m)

Alternanthera 'Aurea Nana' (x 150 per sq yd/per sq m)

Alternanthera 'Brilliantissima' (x 150 per sq yd/per sq m)

Alternanthera 'Versicolor' (x 150 per sq yd/per sq m)

Dudleya farinosa (x 12 per yd/per m)

The real skill with bedding displays is devising the design. Simple shapes can be very effective and bold; by contrast, a complicated design will sit very well in a knot garden. A personal emblem or figurative elements such as butterflies and birds can be incorporated into a design. Bedding plants are short-lived, so there is room for experimentation.

plants

Annuals are not the only kind of bedding plant; there are countless others that work just as well, including perennials, succulents, and houseplants. Think of the colors and textures you require, then look for the best candidates.

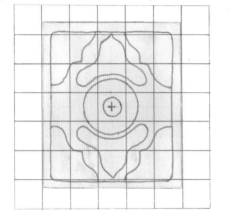

planning a design

If the design is complicated, work it out to scale on graph paper to get the proportions right and to calculate how many plants will be needed. This design is 10 x 20 ft (3 x 6 m), but it can be adapted to the size of your garden.

marking out the design

Prepare the soil, then mark out the design on the surface using light-colored sand. The grid from your paper plan can be transferred using strings or lengths of wood.

planting the bed

Assemble all your plants, making sure you have enough to complete the job. Starting from the middle of the bed or border and working out to the edges, plant the design. Use a plank if necessary as a bridge from which to work. Trim and neaten the plants as you go, because you may not be able to reach the center again.

planting scheme

1 *Cordyline australis* (x 1)

2 *Echeveria pulvinata* (x 8 per yd/per m)

3 *Echeveria secunda* var. *glauca* (x 8 per yd/per m)

4 *Sedum acre* (x 150 per sq yd/per sq m)

5 *Echeveria elegans* (x 10 per yd/per m)

6 *Alternanthera* 'Aurea Nana' (x 150 per sq yd/per sq m)

7 *Alternanthera* 'Brilliantissima' (x 150 per sq yd/per sq m)

8 *Alternanthera* 'Versicolor' (x 150 per sq yd/per sq m)

9 *Dudleya farinosa* (x 12 per yd/per m)

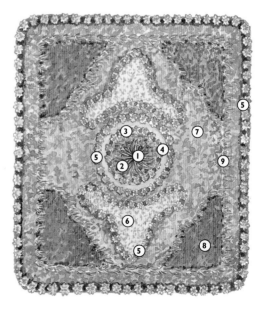

a modern touch

Carpet beds are often viewed as old-fashioned, but the wealth of plants available today and the preference for clear-cut graphic planting make bedding ideal. A group of small beds will enliven the smallest city courtyard. Look for inspiration beyond the garden, in books on tapestry, cross-stitch, or quilting (below and right).

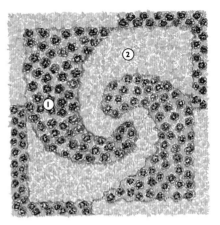

square bed

1 *Tagetes* Bonanza Series
 (x 36 per sq yd/per sq m)
2 *Tagetes* 'Vanilla'
 (x 25 per sq yd/per sq m)

diamond bed

1 *Viola cornuta* 'Victoria Cawthorne'
 (x 25 per sq yd/per sq m)
2 *Viola* 'Ardross Gem' (x 25 per sq yd/per sq m)
3 *Viola pedata* (x 25 per sq yd/per sq m)
4 *Viola* 'Huntercombe Purple' (x 25 per sq yd/per sq m)

care and maintenance

- Tender plants, as here, should not be planted until the threat of frost has passed.
- Keep the bed weed free.
- Preserve or propagate plants for use the following year.

foliage bed

Foliage has a great advantage over flowers: It is present for most of the growing season
or, in the case of evergreens, throughout the year. A foliage garden or border need
never be boring. It can be a very cool, restful place, especially if the colors, shapes,
and textures have been grouped in a sympathetic manner. By contrast and for
a flamboyant touch, there are exotic and brightly colored foliage plants to
create a party atmosphere and huge-leaved plants to add drama.

PLANTING SCHEME

Phytolacca americana (x 1)

Cornus controversa 'Variegata' (x 1)

Geranium macrorrhizum (x 7)

Polystichum setiferum (x 1)

Geranium palmatum (x 3)

Geranium × *magnificum* (x 3)

Iris sibirica (x 3)

Lysimachia ciliata 'Firecracker' (x 1)

Meconopsis cambrica (x 6)

Euphorbia characias subsp. *wulfenii* (x 3)

Macleaya cordata (x 3)

Romneya coulteri (x 2)

Lysichiton americanus (x 1)

Kniphofia 'Painted Lady' (x 1)

Crocosmia × *crocosmiiflora* 'Solfaterre' (x 3)

Hosta lancifolia (x 1)

Heuchera micrantha var. *diversifolia* 'Palace
Purple' (x 3)

Hosta Tardiana Group 'Halcyon' (x 3)

Euphorbia dulcis 'Chameleon' (x 1)

Miscanthus sinensis (x 1)

Ferula communis (x 1)

Rodgersia podophylla (x 1)

Silybum marianum (x 3)

Since all plants have leaves in one form or another, there are no limits to the mood and effect that can be created using foliage. Some plants, such as hostas and grasses, are used primarily for foliage; for the wealth of plants where flowers are prominent, blooms must be an asset to the green scheme.

foliage forms

When choosing plants, look at the shapes of the leaves as well as their color. A mixture of shapes is usually much more interesting than a multiplication of a single leaf form, although other qualities in the leaf—fleshy or fine, shiny or matte—should also be considered for a well-blended planting, as in this square bed, 18 x 18 ft (5.5 x 5.5 m).

planting scheme

1 *Phytolacca americana* (x 1)
2 *Cornus controversa* 'Variegata' (x 1)
3 *Geranium macrorrhizum* (x 7)
4 *Polystichum setiferum* (x 1)
5 *Geranium palmatum* (x 3)
6 *Geranium* × *magnificum* (x 3)
7 *Iris sibirica* (x 3)
8 *Lysimachia ciliata* 'Firecracker' (x 1)
9 *Meconopsis cambrica* (x 6)
10 *Euphorbia characias* subsp. *wulfenii* (x 3)
11 *Macleaya cordata* (x 3)
12 *Romneya coulteri* (x 2)
13 *Lysichiton americanus* (x 1)
14 *Kniphofia* 'Painted Lady' (x 1)
15 *Crocosmia* × *crocosmiiflora* 'Solfaterre' (x 3)
16 *Hosta lancifolia* (x 1)
17 *Heuchera micrantha* var. *diversifolia* 'Palace Purple' (x 3)
18 *Hosta* Tardiana Group 'Halcyon' (x 3)
19 *Euphorbia dulcis* 'Chameleon' (x 1)
20 *Miscanthus sinensis* (x 1)
21 *Ferula communis* (x 1)
22 *Rodgersia podophylla* (x 1)
23 *Silybum marianum* (x 3)

alternative scheme: silver and blue bed

There are many colors beyond shades of green that can be used in a foliage scheme, and one of the most restful is silver. Many silver and gray plants have soft foliage and a loose, spreading growing pattern that is ideal for an asymmetrical scheme, but also work very well in a more formal planting, as in this example.

combining colors

In this design, pale blue and light pink flowers complement the silver foliage, lifting the overall impression made by the bed without detracting from the delicacy of the foliage shades.

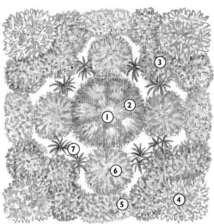

alternative planting

1 *Pyrus salicifolia* 'Pendula' (x 1)
2 *Artemisia* 'Powis Castle' (x 7)
3 *Nepeta* × *faassenii* (x 12)
4 *Stachys byzantina* (x 12)
5 *Dianthus* 'Inchmery' (x 12)
6 *Veronica spicata* subsp. *incana* (x 4)
7 *Nerine bowdenii* (x 16)

other colored foliage

Silver is one of the few colors other than green that will sustain an entire foliage scheme. Purple foliage is very bold when it punctuates a green planting but dull if massed, as are gold and bronze. Variegated plants can add confusion if used without restraint. However, all are excellent as foliage highlights.

care and maintenance

- Remove any spent flowering stems, leaving the foliage to provide the interest. The foliage of *Geranium magnificum* should be cut after flowering to encourage a fresh crop of leaves.
- In fall remove any dead foliage and top-dress with organic matter. Tie up the kniphofia foliage in a bunch above the crown to protect it.
- In spring remove any remaining old foliage, including that of the ferns and the kniphofia.

mixed border

The use of mixed plantings has become the favorite form of ornamental gardening. Shrubs combined with perennials give a bed a sense of permanence and structure that lasts throughout the year, even during the winter months. Spring bulbs provide drifts of color and annuals make valuable contributions—they can be changed each year, thereby altering the general appearance of the border, they quickly fill gaps, and their bright colors add a touch of gaiety.

PLANTING SCHEME

Primula 'Blue Riband' (x 5)

Papaver somniferum (x 4)

Rosa gallica var. *officinalis* 'Versicolor' (x 1)

Aruncus dioicus (x 1)

Pyrus salicifolia 'Pendula' (x 1)

Delphinium 'Fenella' (x 2)

Salvia forsskaolii (x 6)

Veronica 'Shirley Blue' (x 2)

Geranium × riversleaianum 'Mavis Simpson' (x 1)

Leymus arenarius (x 1)

Dianthus 'Doris' (x 3)

Sisyrinchium striatum (x 4)

Baptisia australis (x 1)

Trifolium rubens (x 1)

Papaver orientale 'Mrs Perry' (x 1)

Silene dioica (x 2)

Lilium regale (x 3)

Campanula persicifolia (x 1)

Salvia sclarea (x 1)

Tanacetum vulgare (x 5)

Viola cornuta (x 3)

A wide range of perennials, shrubs, and annuals can be used in this type of border. Try to use plants that are complementary in color and texture. Beyond the short-term presence of bulbs and the changing interest given by annuals, it is very satisfying to watch a mixed bed or border mature and develop over the years. Make allowance for growth when you plan and plant.

maintenance considerations

Mixed beds can require more attention than, say, the perennial or annual bed. It is possible to select plants that need little attention, but this eliminates some of the most rewarding plants that do need to be pruned, divided, and protected against the elements. Decide how much time you can give to a bed before selecting the plants.

confining the leymus

Leymus is a fine plant but it spreads rapidly. Plant it in a large pot and then plunge this into the border so the rim is level with the top of the soil. Renew the soil every year.

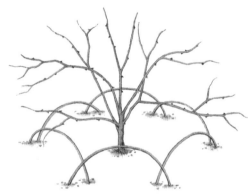

confining shrub roses

If shrub roses are left to their own devices not only do they become rather loose and open in appearance but their long stems can be swept up by winds, damaging adjacent plants.

They can be controlled by tying the branches down; bending the stems also promotes flowering. Using pliable sticks, create a circle of overlapping hoops around the rose (above), then tie the long shoots in (right).

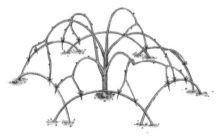

Each stem should be secured to the hoops while retaining a natural arched shape. New growth will soon hide the circle of sticks. Take the structure apart each spring, prune, and retie. Remove a few of the older stems at the base to help promote new, vigorous growth.

a corner bed

This corner planting,
10 x 15 ft (3 x 4.5 m),
makes a fine feature in
the garden, set off by
a clipped hedge.

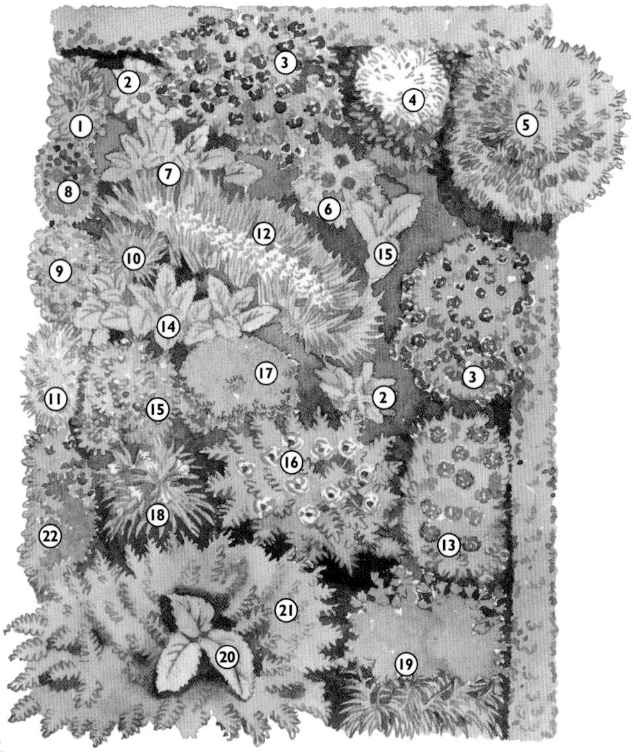

planting scheme

1 *Primula* 'Blue Riband' (x 5)
2 *Papaver somniferum* (x 4)
3 *Rosa gallica* var. *officinalis*
  'Versicolor' (x 1)
4 *Aruncus dioicus* (x 1)
5 *Pyrus salicifolia* 'Pendula' (x 1)
6 *Delphinium* 'Fenella' (x 2)
7 *Salvia forsskaolii* (x 3)
8 *Veronica* 'Shirley Blue' (x 2)
9 *Geranium* × *riversleaianum*
  'Mavis Simpson' (x 1)
10 *Leymus arenarius* (x 1)
11 *Dianthus* 'Doris' (x 3)
12 *Sisyrinchium striatum* (x 4)
13 *Baptisia australis* (x 1)
14 *Salvia forsskaolii* (x 3)
15 *Trifolium rubens* (x 1)
16 *Papaver orientale* 'Mrs Perry'
  (x 1)
17 *Silene dioica* (x 2)
18 *Lilium regale* (x 3)
19 *Campanula persicifolia* (x 1)
20 *Salvia sclarea* (x 1)
21 *Tanacetum vulgare* (x 5)
22 *Viola cornuta* (x 3)

care and maintenance

• In spring, support the
  Papaver orientale. Other
  tall plants such as the
  Tanacetum, *Baptisia*,
  Campanula, and
  Delphinium should also be
  supported in windy areas.
• Cutting off withered portions will
  promote flowering and mimimize
  undesirable seeding.
• In fall, cut back all dead and dying
  herbaceous material, remove weeds,
  and top-dress with organic matter.
• In early spring, prune the roses and cut out
  any dead wood that can be seen on the pear.

purple and yellow

Color, both of flowers and foliage, influences the mood as well as the general appearance of a garden. Cool, pastel shades create a romantic, tranquil feel; hot colors add excitement and a sense of the exotic. Borders can be designed to contain a mixture of colors or to use a more restrained range to striking ends. A single color makes a strong impression, but two complementary or contrasting colors can produce some of the most remarkable effects.

PLANTING SCHEME

Ligustrum lucidum 'Aureum' (x 1)

Asphodeline lutea (x 3)

Allium hollandicum (x 6)

Allium cristophii (x 3)

Helianthus 'Lemon Queen' (x 1)

Anthemis tinctoria (x 1)

Oenothera stricta (x 3)

Rosa glauca (x 1)

Cynara cardunculus (x 1)

Lupinus arboreus (x 1)

Atriplex hortensis var. *rubra* (x 3)

Kniphofia 'Yellow Hammer' (x 1)

Lobelia × *gerardii* 'Vedrariensis' (x 3)

Verbascum olympicum (x 1)

Heuchera sanguinea (x 3)

Euphorbia × *martinii* (x 3)

For a two-color border, choose the plants carefully. It may be best to plan the border over several seasons, carrying a notebook to jot down suitable plants as you see them in other gardens. Shrubs, perennials, annuals, and grasses can all be used to good effect; take cuttings or divide plants to ensure that the color will remain consistent. This 6 x 15 ft (1.8 x 4.5 m) border has year-round interest.

selecting colors

Choosing colors is a personal matter; we all have our favorites and dislikes. But before two colors are selected, certain factors should be considered. Does the combination work or jar? There are certainly many pairings that are not as successful as others, such as red and white or orange and purple. Can the shades of the chosen plants be restricted effectively? For example, using every tone of pink could be busy enough without adding another color. And does the combination create the desired mood?

planting scheme

1 *Ligustrum lucidum* 'Aureum' (x 1)

2 *Asphodeline lutea* (x 3)

3 *Allium hollandicum* (x 6)

4 *Allium cristophii* (x 3)

5 *Helianthus* 'Lemon Queen' (x 1)

6 *Anthemis tinctoria* (x 1)

7 *Oenothera stricta* (x 3)

8 *Rosa glauca* (x 1)

9 *Cynara cardunculus* (x 1)

10 *Lupinus arboreus* (x 1)

11 *Atriplex hortensis* var. *rubra* (x 3)

12 *Kniphofia* 'Yellow Hammer' (x 1)

13 *Lobelia* × *gerardii* 'Vedrariensis' (x 3)

14 *Verbascum olympicum* (x 1)

15 *Heuchera sanguinea* (x 3)

16 *Euphorbia* × *martinii* (x 3)

care and maintenance

- Cut the lupines back to the ground when they have finished flowering, or just remove the old flower spikes to encourage a second crop of smaller flowers.
- Cut the anthemis to the ground after flowering to encourage fresh foliage.
- Allow the self-sowing annuals and biennials limited time to seed to prevent overcrowding. Thin the resulting seedlings as they emerge.
- Cut back dead foliage in fall.
- Tie the kniphofia leaves in a bunch over the crown of the plant for winter protection and then cut the leaves away in spring as the new foliage emerges.
- Top-dress in the winter with well-rotted organic material.

spring planting

To provide interest in early spring, plant daffodils and dark-colored tulips between the existing planting. The emerging herbaceous foliage will cover the bulbs' dying leaves, which can also be cut off once they begin to turn brown.

other partners for yellow

Yellow is one of the most versatile colors in the garden. It represents a huge section of garden plants and works very well with other colors, in different ways.

pruning

The *Rosa glauca* in this border can be pruned heavily each spring, removing the old wood almost to the ground. This looks drastic but will encourage new shoots with masses of richly colored foliage.

yellow and blue

1 *Anthemis tinctoria*
2 *Helianthus* 'Lemon Queen'
3 *Kniphofia* 'Yellow Hammer'
4 *Oenothera stricta*
5 *Verbascum olympicum*
6 *Aquilegia flabellata*
7 *Eryngium × tripartitum*
8 *Aster frikartii*
9 *Delphinium* hybrids
10 *Veronica* 'Shirley Blue'
11 *Veronica longifolia*

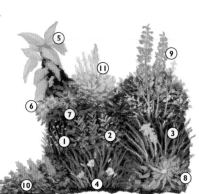

yellow and orange

1 *Anthemis tinctoria*
2 *Helianthus* 'Lemon Queen'
3 *Kniphofia* 'Yellow Hammer'
4 *Oenothera stricta*
5 *Verbascum olympicum*
6 *Canna* 'Orange Perfection'
7 *Crocosmia × crocosmiiflora* 'Emily McKenzie'
8 *Dahlia* 'Bishop of Llandaff'
9 *Euphorbia griffithii* 'Fireglow'
10 *Geum* 'Borisii'
11 *Papaver atlanticum*

left The shapes of beds are better defined if they are outlined by a low hedge which prevents the plants flopping over the edge.

right A combination of paths and hedges weaves a tapestry in this cottage garden. The low, contained planting enhances the shapes.

shaped borders

are rewarding to create; almost any shape can be used, whether geometric or free-flowing, although sharp points are difficult to plant unless they have first been lined with a low hedge. Circular beds have elegance, a sinuous border has charm; a parterre is the ultimate expression of order and complexity.

far left Curved, meandering lines to a border are much more interesting than a straight edge, especially when the planting is informal, as here.

above left A simple or symmetrical design featuring a central plant or ornament uses a circular bed to best advantage.

below left A clean edge between a planted border and an area of grass always helps to enhance the shape of the border.

left Large patterned areas can be most effective, especially if they can be viewed from above, as from the raised walkway over this delightful, well-planned parterre.

below left The use of shaped borders is a good approach to designing single-colored gardens. Here, the shapes fit perfectly into the available space and set off the pattern of the brick path.

below right A circular rose bed surrounded by a gravel path—a picturesque corner of a fine garden. Small hedges extend into the circle, leading the eye toward the birdbath in the middle, an imaginative, witty device.

35

round bed

To many people the words "border" and "bed" conjure up the image of a long strip of cultivated ground, but in fact there is no reason why a planted space should not be any shape. One of the most popular is a round bed, situated in the middle of a lawn or surrounded by a path. The symmetry of a circle is particularly effective in a formal garden; a classical approach is a group of four circular beds. By contrast, filled with annuals, the bed becomes a very cheerful, informal feature.

PLANTING SCHEME

Allium cristophii (x 1)

Artemisia alba 'Canescens' (x 10)

Milium effusum (x 5)

Rosa 'Ballerina' (x 5)

Scabiosa caucasica 'Clive Greaves' (x 5)

Viola, mixed pink and blue (numerous)

There are several ways of planting a round bed, depending on its role in the garden. In an informal setting, a border of mixed plants, randomly planted, can look very effective. For a formal design, order is the essential element, often with a central axis; a standard rose, planted urn, or piece of statuary.

creating the circle

There is a simple method for marking out a circular bed. Place a stake or strong stick where the center is to be. Tie a length of string to this and at the desired radius tie another stick. Keeping the string taut, walk around, scoring a circle in the ground.

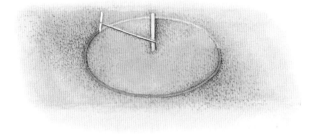

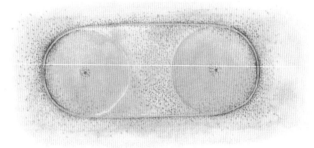

creating an oval

Another pleasing bed shape is an oval. This is easily marked out by outlining two circles (as above) and joining them with straight lines. When planning the length of such a bed, remember that the radius of the circles is an important measurement. Use a tall plant at the center of each "circle."

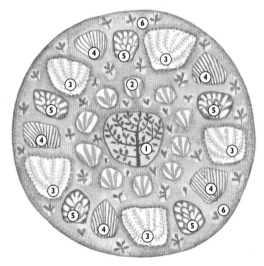

planting

As with all symmetrical schemes, the rule is to start at the center and work outward. Plan the bed on paper first; even a small bed can take a lot of undoing if things go wrong. This example measures 10 ft (3 m) across.

planting scheme

1 *Allium cristophii* (x 1)
2 *Artemisia alba* 'Canescens' (x 10)
3 *Milium effusum* (x 5)
4 *Rosa* 'Ballerina' (x 5)
5 *Scabiosa caucasica* 'Clive Greaves' (x 5)
6 *Viola*, mixed pink and blue (numerous)

ideas for round beds

The simplest solution, well suited to a formal garden, is a bed devoted almost entirely to one variety of plant, perhaps with a single tree or bush in the center and a low boxwood hedge or edging around the perimeter. Alternatively, for a more contemporary look, a bold pattern can be created using bedding plants: a jagged gash of color across the bed or a series of concentric circles.

alternative planting

1 *Stachys byzantina* (x 4)
2 *Salvia patens* (x 60)
3 *Salvia fulgens* (x 60)
4 *Heliotropium arborescens*
  'P. K. Lowther' (x 60)

alternative scheme: a wheel

One of the most effective ways to plant a round bed is to create a spoked wheel, with a central pivot, radiating bands, and planted "spaces," and an edging, each containing a single variety of plant. Use color wisely, with a restricted palette of complementary tones.

care and maintenance

- With closely planted beds such as these, it is important to keep plant growth neat, otherwise the bed can look crowded and unkempt.
- Step carefully to cause minimal disturbance when pruning a standard rose or topiary centerpiece.

parterre

Although parterres may seem appropriate only to stately homes, many a small town
garden contains one, scaled down and designed to enhance the size and shape available.
In essence, a parterre is a formal arrangement of beds to create a geometric or more
fluid pattern. Typically, the edges are delineated by low hedges or brickwork, with
the enclosed spaces filled with plants of contrasting colors. The results are pleasing
to the eye and at their best provide year-round interest.

PLANTING SCHEME

Buxus sempervirens 'Suffruticosa' (9 per yd/per m)
Sedum 'Herbstfreude' (4 per sq yd/per sq m)
Begonia × carrierei 'Red Ascot' (36 per sq yd/per sq m)
Nicotiana langsdorffii (9 per sq yd/per sq m)
Verbena 'Blue Lagoon' (9 per sq yd/per sq m)

There is no right or wrong way to create a parterre. A designer's imagination can run free, making the pattern as simple or as complicated as he or she wants. Although curves soften a design, an entirely straight-edged parterre can be very successful. Much of the overall impact of a parterre lies in the viewing and it will always be more impressive if viewed from above, from a terrace or window.

a formal parterre

Much of the challenge in producing a beautiful traditional parterre lies in the plant selection. Starting with the framework, the best growing border is dwarf boxwood, but other good candidates include lavender—with the bonus of its fragrance—santolina, and teucrium. Traditionally, each bed should be made up of plants of a single color or sometimes two colors. Annuals allow for and demand a yearly change; small shrubs form a permanent planting. High on the list should come snapdragons, begonias, diascias, lobelias, impatiens, salvias, and pansies. Parterres do not have to be large. This one is 15 x 20 ft (4.5 x 6 m).

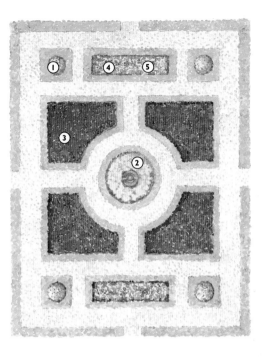

planting scheme

1 *Buxus sempervirens* 'Suffruticosa' (9 per yd/per m)

2 *Sedum* 'Herbstfreude' (4 per sq yd/per sq m)

3 *Begonia* × *carrierei* 'Red Ascot' (36 per sq yd/ per sq m)

4 *Nicotiana langsdorffii* (9 per sq yd/per sq m)

5 *Verbena* 'Blue Lagoon' (9 per sq yd/per sq m)

care and maintenance

- Keep the boxwood well trimmed.
- Keep gravel paths well raked.
- Do not make the contained beds too large, otherwise planting and trimming will be very difficult.

brick parterre

In marked, and some might say refreshing, contrast to traditional planted parterres are brick-based designs. These are ideal for smaller city gardens and are the answer for anyone seeking the order and impact of a parterre without waiting years to see hedging at its best. Much of the interest lies in the pattern of the brickwork but by no means all. The same principle applies as for planted parterres when filling beds. Use blocks of color or single plants. If space is limited, a clever and witty approach is to fill the compartments with vegetables and herbs. In this way, a modern courtyard can become a traditional herb garden.

alternative planting

1 onions
2 Swiss chard
3 lettuce
4 chives
5 leeks
6 parsley
7 Brussels sprouts
8 beets
9 cabbages
10 red lettuce
11 bok-choy
12 zucchini
13 radishes
14 pole beans
15 carrots

shapes

Parterres have taken all manner of shapes over the centuries. Favorite devices are trompe l'oeil effects, with "overlapping" beds and dynamic curlicues. All were conceived in the name of elegance, formality, style, and wit.

corner planting

All gardens have odd corners, and since most gardeners complain that they never have enough space, it makes sense to use all these pockets. Another advantage of filling these corners is that it helps to unify the garden, to create an overall picture. A common solution is to use bland ground-cover plants to fill such areas, but it is far better to create something interesting like this simple, cool-looking border. Make every inch count.

PLANTING SCHEME

Alchemilla alpina (x 9)

Euphorbia stricta (x 4)

Mimulus guttatus (x 3)

Deschampsia flexuosa (x 2)

Geranium pratense 'Mrs Kendall Clark' (x 1)

Alchemilla conjuncta (x 1)

One way to deal with small corners is to fill them with containers of plants, but while this is useful in paved areas, there is far less work—particularly when watering—if the plants are put into a properly prepared bed. Often awkwardly shaped, corner beds need to be treated with particular imagination. They will then play their part in the whole garden picture.

a gravel finish

Gravel is a very useful garden material. It is a mulch, complements many plants and presents an orderly finish. It can make a highlight of a corner planting, as in this 12 x 12 ft (3.5 x 3.5 m) plot. Alternatively, use concrete pavers and plant between them, creating a tapestry of cover. Erigeron, acaena, thyme, and mint are useful; the last two are aromatic.

care and maintenance

- If planting close to a wall, avoid using tall plants that may bend forward, drawn to the light and pushed by winds.
- Make sure the gravel is well distributed around the plants and that any small rocks are stable.

planting scheme
1 *Alchemilla alpina* (x 9)
2 *Euphorbia stricta* (x 4)
3 *Mimulus guttatus* (x 3)
4 *Deschampsia flexuosa* (x 2)
5 *Geranium pratense* 'Mrs Kendall Clark' (x 1)
6 *Alchemilla conjuncta* (x 1)

alternative scheme: a small rock garden

A well-constructed, well-planted rock garden is an excellent solution for many corners. The rule is to bury at least half of each rock in the soil—this will secure it and provide a cool, moist root-run. Arrange rocks in tiers, all leaning back slightly.

safety considerations

Never lift more than you can comfortably handle and protect your fingers from crushing stones. Get help if necessary. Move large rocks using a strong pole as a lever or roll rather than lift them. Make sure all rocks are stable.

alternative planting scheme

1 *Daphne tangutica* (x 1)

2 *Juniperus communis* 'Compressa' (x 1)

3 *Picea mariana* 'Nana' (x 1)

4 *Helianthemum* 'Annabel' (x 1)

5 *Phlox douglasii* 'Crackerjack' (x 1)

6 *Aubrieta* 'Joy' (x 1)

7 *Euphorbia myrsinites* (x 1)

8 *Lewisia tweedyi* (x 2)

9 *Erinus alpinus* (x 1)

10 *Dianthus* 'Little Jock' (x 1)

11 *Rhodohypoxis baurii* (x 10)

12 *Armeria juniperifolia* (x 1)

13 *Pulsatilla vulgaris* (x 1)

14 *Androsace carnea* subsp. *laggeri* (x 1)

15 *Achillea clavennae* (x 1)

16 *Gentiana septemfida* (x 1)

17 *Convolvulus althaeoides* (x 1)

18 *Sisyrinchium idahoense* subsp. *bellum* (x 1)

19 *Hypericum olympicum* 'Citrinum' (x 1)

20 *Campanula carpatica* (x 1)

21 *Aster alpinus* (x 1)

22 *Geranium cinereum* subsp. *subcaulescens* (x 1)

23 *Dianthus* 'Annabel' (x 1)

24 *Polygala chamaebuxus* var. *grandiflora* (x 1)

25 *Erodium corsicum* (x 3)

designing a rock garden

Rock gardens are intended to replicate rocky outcrops, so aim for layers of rocks that are similar in size but not too orderly.

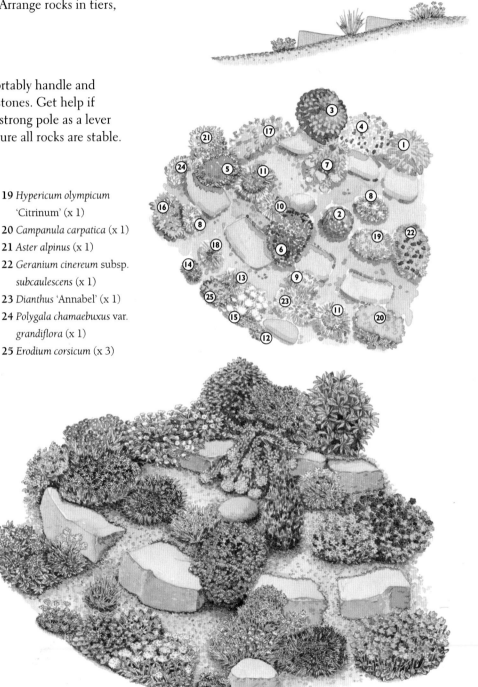

care and maintenance

- Weed rock gardens regularly; once weeds have taken hold, they can be difficult to remove.
- The top-dressing of gravel will gradually mix into the soil; replace it as necessary.
- Cover any plants that may suffer from winter cold with a sheet of glass or a frame covered with plastic, but allow air to circulate at the sides.
- Water alpines during dry spells.
- Trim back straggling plants.

special borders

give the garden a distinctive and often unusual character. From enlivening dry and shaded sites to lifting a pond display, these borders often include plants and materials that are quite different from those seen in traditional beds.

left Waterside planting can include an exuberant mixture of foliage and flowering plants, presenting luxuriant displays. Here, white lilies shine out against clumps of spreading foliage.

right Candelabra primulas are extremely good plants for wet and boggy areas. Both their color and shape create interest and are seen at their best against still, bright water.

below Some wetland plants, such as this *Iris ensata*, can be grown in an ordinary border if a pond is not available, as long as they have plenty of moisture-retaining soil.

above Shady and woodland borders have a peaceful, protected quality. Hellebores, hepaticas, and cyclamen are all ideal for such conditions.

above left Grasses are wonderful plants for the varied form and color of their foliage and for their sheer versatility and hardiness. They are an asset in dry beds.

above right Succulent plants, such as this spiny agave, will thrive in dry Mediterranean-style growing conditions. Gravel creates a perfect background for drought-tolerant plants, particularly architectural specimens that deserve space to be admired.

center A subtle variation in colors is always worth trying. The result can be very cool and satisfying, as in this healthy dry border in shades of green and yellow.

right In areas where rainfall has declined it is essential to change to plants that will grow happily in dry conditions. The diversity of suitable plants, often very dramatic in appearance, confirms that a dry climate does not mean dull gardens.

waterside planting

Water features add a special dimension to a garden. A soothing sound as a stream
trickles or a pool ripples, lively or leisurely movement and subtle reflections or
darts of light; all are irresistible to any gardener. Such features allow and call for
a lush planting of fresh colors, both in the flowers and the foliage. The whole
environment around a water feature creates a tranquillity that is rarely
reproduced elsewhere in the garden.

MATERIALS AND EQUIPMENT

spade

soft builder's sand

PVC or butyl membrane pond liner to size

bricks

pieces of sod

topsoil

compost

plants for the ledge (see right)

perforated pots for planting in the pond

PLANTING SCHEME

Iris pseudacorus 'Variegata' (x 1)

Iris sibirica (x 6)

Ranunculus lingua (x 5)

Phalaris arundinacea (x 3)

Typha latifolia (x 3)

Hosta sieboldiana var. *elegans* (x 1)

Hosta tokudama f. *flavocircinalis* (x 1)

Mimulus luteus (x 3)

Hydrocharis morsus-ranae (x 3)

Nymphaea 'René Gérard' (x 1)

Primula pulverulenta (x 2)

Salix babylonica (x 1)

Although many of the plants grown beside a pond can also be grown in a border, most particularly enjoy moist soil. Avoid plants that prefer dry conditions—this includes most silver-foliaged plants. Those intended to grow in shallow water at the edge and in the pond should be true aquatic plants.

creating a waterside border

Dig out the pond to the shape required, including a ledge around the edge; this will carry the waterside border. Slope the ledge outward to encourage the absorption of water from the pool. Cover the whole surface with a layer of soft builder's sand to about 2 in (5 cm) in depth to prevent sharp objects from penetrating the liner.

lining the pond and border

Stretch the liner across the pond so that it extends well beyond the ledge. Place bricks around the edge to keep it stretched, then fill the pond. The liner will sink, taking up the profile of the hole, dragging the bricks inward. Fill the liner to the edge of the ledge. Ease the material into the contours of the ledge and tuck the liner firmly into the bank so that it is concealed.

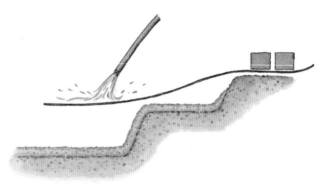

making the border

Build a wall of inverted pieces of sod, forming a bank. Fill the space behind this with a mixture of topsoil and compost. Allow the soil to settle, then add more water to the pond so that it soaks into the border. If the soil in the border sinks, top it off.

planting the bed

When planting an edging bed on top of a liner, be careful not to damage the material when digging. Carefully dig holes and insert the plants. Plant those that require most water, or that will grow with their roots in water, at the edge of the pond. To add variety to the scheme, suitable plants can be placed in the pond itself in special perforated pots. This full design is 10 x 20 ft (3 x 6 m).

planting scheme

1 *Iris pseudacorus* 'Variegata' (x 1)

2 *Iris sibirica* (x 6)

3 *Ranunculus lingua* (x 5)

4 *Phalaris arundinacea* (x 3)

5 *Typha latifolia* (x 3)

6 *Hosta sieboldiana* var. *elegans*
   (x 1)

7 *Hosta tokudama* f. *flavocircinalis*
   (x 1)

8 *Mimulus luteus* (x 3)

9 *Hydrocharis morsus-ranae* (x 3)

10 *Nymphaea* 'René Gérard' (x 1)

11 *Primula pulverulenta* (x 2)

12 *Salix babylonica* (x 1)

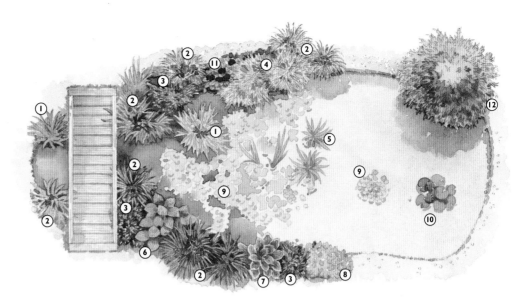

care and maintenance

- Weeds love lush, moist conditions and must be removed constantly, otherwise they can overrun a waterside planting, making it look neglected.
- Cut back dead foliage in autumn and top-dress the edging bed with organic matter such as compost or leaf mold.
- Many waterside plants are invasive and need to be thinned out every two or three years. Replant just a few pieces.
- When maintaining the border, be careful not to puncture the liner.
- Check the condition of the liner regularly, looking for any exposed or damaged areas.

dry border

Gardeners throughout the world are facing a shortage of water, so it is a good idea to make the most of plants that are used to growing in dry regions. Just as attractive as plants from temperate areas, their more defined growth habits and foliage forms can give a border a striking, architectural appearance. For a neat finish, the ground can be mulched with small stones. These will help preserve moisture and keep down weeds, making the border easy to maintain.

TOOLS AND MATERIALS

spade

tamper or roller

large stones for underlayer

small stones for path

path edging (optional)

PLANTING SCHEME

Penstemon heterophyllus (x 5)

Asphodeline lutea (x 3)

Persicaria affinis (x 5)

Juniperus scopulorum
'Skyrocket' (x 1)

Eryngium giganteum (x 8)

Stipa gigantea (x 1)

Sedum 'Vera Jameson' (x 3)

Phormium tenax (x 1)

Artemisia 'Powis Castle' (x 1)

Verbena bonariensis (x 7)

Sedum telephium subsp.
maximum 'Atropurpureum'
(x 3)

Allium hollandicum 'Purple
Sensation' (x 7)

Stachys byzantina (x 3)

Pennisetum villosum (x 1)

Agapanthus 'Ben Hope' (x 1)

Euphorbia dulcis 'Chameleon'
(x 3)

The beauty of drought-tolerant plants is that they need very little attention once established. For the best results, dig over the empty bed in the autumn, adding well-rotted organic material to improve the soil and some sharp sand or fine grit. Together, these additions will help to lighten the soil. Any rain should then rapidly soak through.

a suitable path

Paths made of gravel or small stones not only make a good surface on which to walk but also provide a good setting for plants that like dry conditions.

making a gravel path

To make a stony path, first remove all weeds and, depending on the size of the path, tamp (right) or roll the surface down for a compact, level finish.

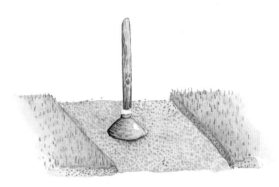

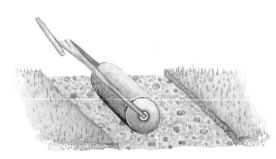

Cover the prepared base with a layer of stones, 1 in (2.5 cm) deep. This should be rolled well into the base (left).

Another method is to dig out the path to a depth of 1–2 in (2.5–5 cm), level it, roll it, and then lay landscape fabric (right). Bury the edges into the soil on either side of the path.

Finally, for both methods, cover with a loose layer of stones at least 1 in (2.5 cm) deep. Edge the path with wood, stone, or bricks (left), or leave the sides vague to merge with the bed.

planting scheme

1 *Penstemon heterophyllus* (x 5)

2 *Asphodeline lutea* (x 3)

3 *Persicaria affinis* (x 5)

4 *Juniperus scopulorum* 'Skyrocket' (x 1)

5 *Eryngium giganteum* (x 8)

6 *Stipa gigantea* (x 1)

7 *Sedum* 'Vera Jameson' (x 3)

8 *Phormium tenax* (x 1)

9 *Artemisia* 'Powis Castle' (x 1)

10 *Verbena bonariensis* (x 7)

11 *Sedum telephium* subsp. *maximum* 'Atropurpureum' (x 3)

12 *Allium hollandicum* 'Purple Sensation' (x 7)

13 *Stachys byzantina* (x 3)

14 *Pennisetum villosum* (x 1)

15 *Agapanthus* 'Ben Hope' (x 1)

16 *Euphorbia dulcis* 'Chameleon' (x 3)

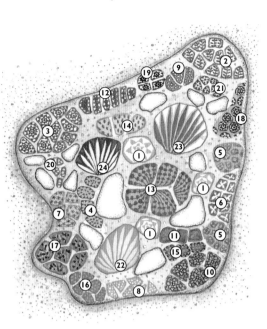

alternative scheme: succulents

Succulents are ideal for dry conditions, giving a garden a healthy display of lush plants, typified by fleshy leaves. As with the main planting, this irregular bed, which is approximately 18 x 18 ft (5.5 x 5.5 m), is surrounded by an informal gravel path.

alternative planting

1 *Cotyledon orbiculata* (x 3)
2 *Dorotheanthus bellidiformis* (x 10)
3 *Jovibarba hirta* (x 10)
4 *Rhodiola rosea* (x 4)
5 *Sedum acre* (x 20)
6 *Sedum aizoon* 'Euphorbioides' (x 8)
7 *Sedum lydium* (x 5)
8 *Sedum spathulifolium* 'Aureum' (x 6)
9 *Sedum spectabile* 'Meteor' (x 3)
10 *Sedum spurium* 'Schorbuser Blut' (x 5)
11 *Sedum telephium* subsp. *maximum* 'Atropurpureum' (x 3)
12 *Sedum* 'Bertram Anderson' (x 6)

13 *Sedum* 'Herbstfreude' (x 5)
14 *Sedum* 'Morchen' (x 3)
15 *Sedum* 'Ruby Glow' (x 3)
16 *Sedum* 'Sunset Cloud' (x 6)
17 *Sedum* 'Vera Jameson' (x 6)
18 *Sempervivum* 'Commander Hay' (x 10)
19 *Sempervivum* 'Glowing Embers' (x 4)
20 *Sempervivum* 'Lady Kelly' (x 5)
21 *Sempervivum tectorum* (x 6)
22 *Yucca flaccida* (x 1)
23 *Yucca gloriosa* 'Variegata' (x 1)
24 *Yucca filamentosa* 'Ivory' (x 1)

care and maintenance

- Be sure that the bed remains well drained.
- Many dry-loving plants produce decorative seed heads that can be kept for autumn interest.

woodland border

Woodland borders conjure up a romantic image of beautiful flowers in wide, misty glades surrounded by luxuriant trees, an image well beyond most gardens. However, the idea can be realized on a much smaller scale with surprising success. Such a border needs only one or two trees to provide the shade and atmosphere while the smaller plants create the effect. Indeed, there is no reason why the whole could not be miniaturized and created under a few large shrubs.

TOOLS AND MATERIALS

spade

tamper or roller

logs

sticks

bark nuggets

PLANTING SCHEME

Rosa 'Ramona' (x 1)

Corylus avellana (x 1)

Hosta Tardiana Group 'Halcyon' (x 1)

Geranium × magnificum (x 3)

Dicentra 'Bountiful' (x 5)

Iris sibirica (x 1)

Geranium pratense (x 1)

Alchemilla mollis (x 2)

Bergenia 'Silberlicht' (x 3)

Brunnera macrophylla (x 1)

Campanula latifolia (x 1)

Digitalis purpurea (x 5)

Epimedium × rubrum (x 1)

Euphorbia amygdaloides var. *robbiae* (x 3)

Helleborus foetidus (x 3)

Myosotis sylvatica (x 3)

Persicaria affinis (x 3)

Pulmonaria officinalis (x 3)

Stylophorum diphyllum (x 2)

Tellima grandiflora (x 3)

Woodland borders extend from under trees where the conditions range from dense to mottled shade. The number of plants that will tolerate full shade is limited, although this is less problematic in spring when the sparser tree canopies allow more light through. For the rest of the year, use the woodland margins to provide color and interest.

woodland conditions

Trees and shrubs are notoriously hungry and thirsty plants, so the soil should be amended with plenty of well-rotted organic material. In keeping with a natural setting, this is best provided by leaf mold made by composting any available foliage after it has fallen in autumn. After clearing any weeds, cultivate the proposed border, adding as much leaf mold as possible. This will help the soil to retain moisture but the border will never be as wet as a bed in open ground, so choose plants that will tolerate dryness. Plant in early autumn on lighter soils but wait until spring if the soil is at all heavy. This border is 15 x 15 ft (4.5 x 4.5 m).

creating a bark path

Paths around a woodland border or through shady areas are best kept informal. A natural material for such paths is bark nuggets, itself a woodland product. This gives a soft finish and particularly suits meandering paths. To make the path, first compact the soil below the intended path (see page 56).

The sides of a bark path can be left vague to blend into the borders or can be edged with logs to prevent the bark from spreading too far. If logs are used, hold them in place by inserting stakes at intervals on either side.

Pour 2–3 in (5–7.5 cm) of bark nuggets along the path. If the layer is deeper than this, the path will be too soft. Rake at regular intervals and top up with fresh bark as the material breaks down into humus.

woodland bulbs

In spring, before the leaves appear on the trees, woodland areas are often full of bulbs, making the most of the sunlight before leafy canopies darken the ground. Many spring bulbs are suitable for woodland use. The best way to achieve a random planting is to broadcast the bulbs onto the ground and plant them where they fall. The depth of planting varies, but as a rule of thumb always plant three times the depth of the bulb.

planting scheme

1 *Rosa* 'Ramona' (x 1)

2 *Corylus avellana* (x 1)

3 *Hosta* Tardiana Group 'Halcyon' (x 1)

4 *Geranium × magnificum* (x 3)

5 *Dicentra* 'Bountiful' (x 5)

6 *Iris sibirica* (x 1)

7 *Geranium pratense* (x 1)

8 *Alchemilla mollis* (x 2)

9 *Bergenia* 'Silberlicht'(x 3)

10 *Brunnera macrophylla* (x 1)

11 *Campanula latifolia* (x 1)

12 *Digitalis purpurea* (x 5)

13 *Epimedium × rubrum* (x 1)

14 *Euphorbia amygdaloides* var. *robbiae* (x 3)

15 *Helleborus foetidus* (x 3)

16 *Myosotis sylvatica* (x 3)

17 *Persicaria affinis* (x 3)

18 *Pulmonaria officinalis* (x 3)

19 *Stylophorum diphyllum* (x 2)

20 *Tellima grandiflora* (x 3)

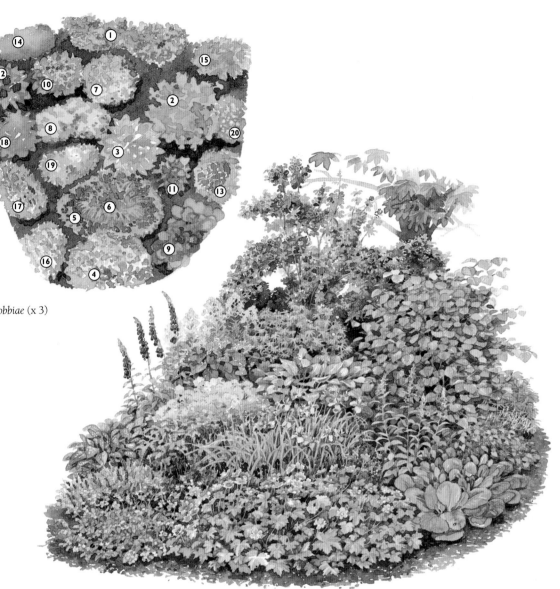

spring underplanting

To enhance spring interest, there are many plants that can be added under and around the main plants. Many of these spring-flowering plants will run to seed, forming a most desirable carpet of color.

spring planting

1 *Anemone nemorosa* (x 4)

2 *Convallaria majalis* (x 4)

3 *Cyclamen coum* (x 8)

4 *Eranthis hyemalis* (x 4)

5 *Galanthus nivalis* (x 20)

6 *Hyacinthoides non-scripta* (x 12)

7 *Narcissus pseudonarcissus* (x 6)

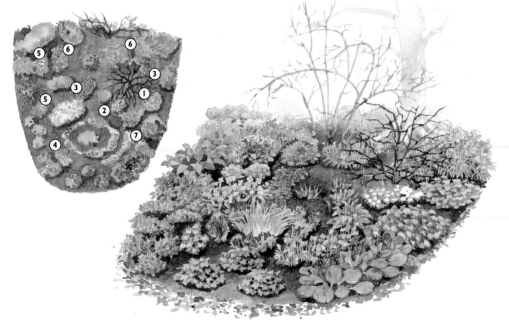

mediterranean border

In areas where hot, dry summers are the norm, there is little point
in trying to create a lush perennial border that prefers cooler conditions.
A Mediterranean border is the ideal solution, with plants that are
colorful in both their flowers and foliage. Hardy plants, they will
succeed in cooler regions where a rather exotic look is desired.

TOOLS AND MATERIALS

spade

tamper or roller

large stones for underlayer

small stones for path

PLANTING SCHEME

Veronica 'Shirley Blue' (x 6)

Cistus × skanbergii (x 1)

Chamaecyparis lawsoniana
'Pembury Blue' (x 1)

Althaea officinalis 'Romney
Marsh' (x 3)

Onopordum acanthium (x 3)

Euphorbia characias (x 1)

Cistus × fernandesiae 'Anne
Palmer' (x 2)

Nectaroscordum siculum (x 25)

Allium unifolium (x 25)

Lavandula officinalis (x 1)

Sedum 'Herbstfreude' (x 3)

Stachys byzantina (x 10)

Ballota pseudodictamnus (x 3)

Salvia × superba 'Superba'
(x 2)

Lychnis coronaria (x 1)

Salvia jurisicii (x 1)

Acaena saccaticupula 'Blue
Haze' (x 12)

Salvia officinalis
'Purpurascens' (x 2)

Linaria purpurea 'Springside
White' (x 1)

Papaver somniferum (x 5)

The Mediterranean border has diversity and warmth of color yet presents quite a different quality from the plants most familiar to temperate climates. They are resilient against dry heat and a surprising degree of cold and make few demands, excellent for low-maintenance gardening.

creating a mediterranean border

Prepare the bed first then lay the path. Work the plot in autumn, removing any perennial weeds and adding well-rotted organic material. Mediterranean plants like ground that does not remain too wet, so if the soil is heavy clay, add sharp sand or fine gravel to help with drainage. In spring, turn over the soil and break it down with a rake, removing any weeds that have appeared over winter. The most suitable pathing is gravel, which can be left to blend with the edges of the bed (see page 56 for construction). This curved site is around 10 x 15 ft (3 x 4.5 m).

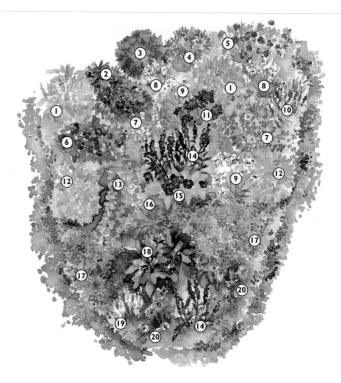

care and maintenance

- Trim back plants after flowering.
- Some of the seed heads such as the *Allium* and the *Onoporum* make good dried flowers and can be kept in the border or picked for indoor use.

planting scheme

1 *Veronica* 'Shirley Blue' (x 6)
2 *Cistus × skanbergii* (x 1)
3 *Chamaecyparis lawsoniana* 'Pembury Blue' (x 1)
4 *Althaea officinalis* 'Romney Marsh' (x 3)
5 *Onopordum acanthium* (x 3)
6 *Euphorbia characias* (x 1)
7 *Cistus × fernandesiae* 'Anne Palmer' (x 2)
8 *Nectaroscordum siculum* (x 25)
9 *Allium unifolium* (x 25)
10 *Lavandula officinalis* (x 1)
11 *Sedum* 'Herbstfreude' (x 3)
12 *Stachys byzantina* (x 10)
13 *Ballota pseudodictamnus* (x 3)
14 *Salvia × superba* 'Superba' (x 2)
15 *Lychnis coronaria* (x 1)
16 *Salvia jurisicii* (x 1)
17 *Acaena saccaticupula* 'Blue Haze' (x 12)
18 *Salvia officinalis* 'Purpurascens' (x 2)
19 *Linaria purpurea* 'Springside White' (x 1)
20 *Papaver somniferum* (x 5)

a dry stream bed

In dry areas the garden can be enhanced by taking elements of the Mediterranean landscape and incorporating them into the border. For example, the impression of a dry stream bed can be created through the center of the border.

dry-stream planting

1 *Miscanthus sinensis* (x 1)

2 *Cordyline australis* (x 1)

3 *Agapanthus* 'Bressingham Blue' (x 1)

4 *Ophiopogon planiscapus* 'Nigrescens' (x 6)

5 *Euphorbia characias* subsp. *wulfenii* (x 1)

6 *Eryngium giganteum* (x 3)

7 *Callistemon citrinus* (x 1)

dry stream planting

The most appropriate design is a sparse planting of grasses and drought-tolerant plants with a jumble of pebbles, smooth rocks, water-worn wood, and old tree stumps lining a shallow gully.

collecting seeds

Many of the plants in this bed produce seeds. When ripe, the seedpods turn brown or black and the seeds fall away freely when lightly moved. Tip the seeds (or seed head) into a labeled paper bag. Place in a warm airy place where the contents of the bag can dry, but not in a hot place and especially not in sunlight. When dry, sift the seeds to remove debris, then empty them into a labeled envelope. This can be kept in the refrigerator until required.

shady border

Many gardens have a shady corner, perhaps in the shadow of an overhanging tree or adjacent walls or fences. In some cases the shade may be dense, in others there may be light from above but the area is never reached by direct sunlight. This situation is one of the most difficult to deal with in gardening terms since most flowering plants need sunshine to do well. However, by rising to the challenge, there are ways of using these areas to advantage.

PLANTING SCHEME

Hosta Tardiana Group 'Halcyon' (x 1)

Hosta fortunei var. *aureomarginata* (x 1)

Euphorbia characias subsp. *wulfenii* (x 1)

Nectaroscordum siculum (x 10)

Nepeta racemosa (x 3)

Tanacetum parthenium (x 6)

Lilium martagon (x 1)

Smyrnium perfoliatum (x 5)

Tellima grandiflora (x 3)

Geranium nedosum (x 1)

Lamium galeobdolon (x 3)

Hemerocallis 'Pink Damask' (x 1)

Dryopteris filix-mas (x 1)

Carex pendula (x 1)

Foeniculum vulgare (x 1)

Hyacinthoides non-scripta (x 10)

Shade usually works hand in hand with other problems. Walls, trees, and similar objects not only cast a sun shadow but a rain shadow; this means that the border is deprived of moisture as well as light. An area between two buildings or structures might also be a drafty location, since whirling currents of air can be created along alleyways even on apparently windless days.

overcoming problems

The right choice of plants will minimize the problem of lack of sunlight, and the moisture content of the soil can be improved by the addition of well-rotted organic material (see page 60) and a mulch. Strong winds can be moderated by using resilient shrubs or a screen as windbreaks. Where part of a border does get the sun, add sun-loving plants; here, in this 6 x 12 ft (1.8 x 3.5 m) bed, nepeta is included.

planting scheme

1 *Hosta* Tardiana Group 'Halcyon' (x 1)
2 *Hosta fortunei* var. *aureomarginata* (x 1)
3 *Euphorbia characias* subsp. *wulfenii* (x 1)
4 *Nectaroscordum siculum* (x 10)
5 *Nepeta racemosa* (x 3)
6 *Tanacetum parthenium* (x 6)
7 *Lilium martagon* (x 1)
8 *Smyrnium perfoliatum* (x 5)
9 *Tellima grandiflora* (x 3)
10 *Geranium nedosum* (x 1)
11 *Lamium galeobdolon* (x 3)
12 *Hemerocallis* 'Pink Damask' (x 1)
13 *Dryopteris filix-mas* (x 1)
14 *Carex pendula* (x 1)
15 *Foeniculum vulgare* (x 1)
16 *Hyacinthoides non-scripta* (x 10)

an ivy corner

A simple but imaginative idea is to fill the shady area with ivy, not in the style of a neglected garden but as a living sculpture. Add surfaces and contours to the space with mounds of earth, tree stumps, or even objects such as old metal chairs, then plant the ivy at 18-in (45-cm) intervals and allow it to ramble freely. The vigorous nature of the plant will come into its own.

other plants for shade

Anemone nemorosa
Arum italicum
Aruncus dioicus
Astilbe
Cardiocrinum giganteum
Convallaria majalis
Cornus canadensis
Corydalis flexuosa
Cyclamen coum
Eranthis hyemalis
Euphorbia amygdaloides
Galanthus nivalis
Helleborus orientalis
Houttuynia cordata
Iris foetidissima
Kirengeshoma palmata
Lathyrus vernus

Lilium martagon
Meconopsis betonicifolia
Omphalodes cappadocica
Omphalodes verna
Oxalis acetosella
Pachysandra terminalis
Polygonatum × hybridum
Primula
Smilacina racemosa
Trillium
Vancouveria chrysantha
Vinca minor
Viola odorata

(see also Woodland Border, pages 58–61)

planting a north wall

Not all gardens can be south- or west-facing, and one of the worst situations in gardening terms is a north wall. This suffers from prolonged or constant shade and, as a result, a marked chilliness when compared to other parts of the same garden. Such an unfavorable microclimate can still support plant life that will cheer a dull corner.

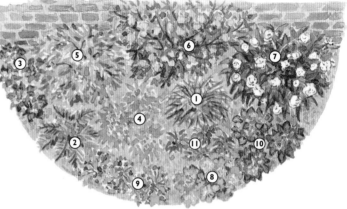

full-shade planting

1 *Carex pendula* (x 1)

2 *Dryopteris filix-mas* (x 1)

3 *Cyclamen hederifolium* (x 5)

4 *Euphorbia amygdaloides*
  var. *robbiae* (x 3)

5 *Garrya elliptica* (x 1)

6 *Rosa* 'New Dawn' (x 1)

7 *Camellia japonica* (x 1)

8 *Alchemilla mollis* (x 1)

9 *Geranium macrorrhizum* (x 3)

10 *Epimedium* × *versicolor*
  'Sulphureum' (x 3)

11 *Hyacinthoides hispanica* (x 4)

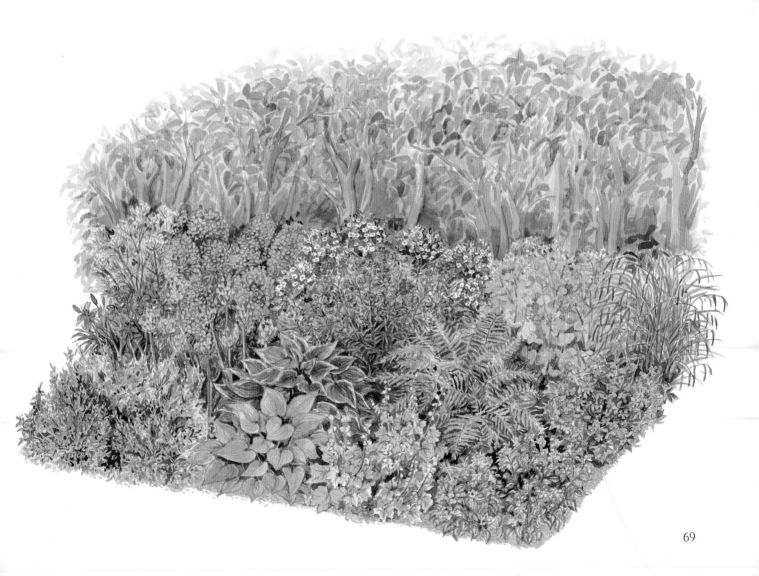

rose bed

Roses are still among the most popular of garden plants. Not only do they provide the garden with masses of beautiful flowers but they also frequently fill it with the most delightful fragrance. Roses are very versatile—they can be used as ground cover, grown as low, medium, or tall bushes, trained around pillars or obelisks, or allowed to scale trellises and even trees. They can be combined with other plants or used by themselves to create a unique feature, the rose garden.

PLANTING SCHEME

Rosa 'Pink Grootendorst' (x 1)
Salvia greggii (x 5)
Geranium palmatum (x 5)

ALTERNATIVE MODERN SHRUB ROSES

'Charles Austin' (apricot and yellow)
'Constance Spry' (pink)
'Cottage Rose' (pink)
'Dark Lady' (deep red)
'English Garden' (yellow)
'Gertrude Jekyll' (pink)

'Glamis Castle' (white)
'Golden Celebration' (yellow)
'Graham Thomas' (yellow)
'Heritage' (pink)
'L. D. Braithwaite' (crimson)
'Mary Rose' (pink)

'Othello' (crimson)
'The Countryman' (pink)
'Warwick Castle' (pink)
'Wife of Bath' (pink)
'Winchester Cathedral' (white)

A rose is such an impressive, complete plant that a bed using a single variety can work very well; if the plant is large then even a single specimen can make a great impact. Here, the large rugosa rose 'Pink Grootendorst' creates a centerpiece around which a small selection of perennials is arranged. These are planted tight against the rose so they merge to form a bold mound.

planting roses

Prepare the soil and plant. Bare-rooted roses should be planted in early spring. This is also the best time for planting container-grown plants, although they can be planted any time if kept watered.

plant associations

Some gardeners like to see bare earth under their roses. However, for an abundant look, there are many plants that work well with roses, including alliums, diascias, anthemises, fragarias, geraniums, persicarias, pulmonarias, stachys, and violas. The best place for these companion plants is around the borders, where they can both be seen and benefit from the sun.

planting scheme

1 *Rosa* 'Pink Grootendorst' (x 1)
2 *Salvia greggii* (x 5)
3 *Geranium palmatum* (x 5)

choosing roses

There are literally thousands of roses to choose from and probably the best way to make a choice is to visit a specialty nursery while they are in flower. Various factors influence a gardener's selection: Flower color and fragrance, whether the plant is repeat-flowering, and the ultimate size of the variety are four key elements. For a relatively confined space, as with this 8-ft (2.4-m) bed, size is a significant point.

alternative modern shrub roses

'Charles Austin'

'Cottage Rose'

'Winchester Cathedral'

'Golden Celebration'

'Heritage'

'Constance Spry'

alternative scheme: an obelisk

Rose beds can consist of just shrub roses or they can include low climbers trained up an obelisk or pillar. More vigorous varieties will swamp a pergola or a long trellis (see page 79). The use of attractive garden structures such as these can enhance the impact of the plants.

alternative planting

1 *Rosa* 'Alister Stella Gray' (x 1)
2 *Rosa* Graham Thomas (x 4)
3 *Tropaeolum majus* 'Alaska' (x 8)

care and maintenance

- To get the best results from roses, prune regularly.
- Be on your guard against diseases, such as blackspot, rust, and powdery mildew, and pests, such as aphids.

walk-through borders

are highly sensuous because they allow the viewer to get among the plants. This creates a greater intimacy with their sight, feel, and smell. Where arches or pergolas are involved, the viewer is totally surrounded by plants and their fragrance. All gardeners should allow time to walk through their borders.

above This very romantic formal paved promenade is lined with borders and contained behind box hedges. The whole is framed by a series of arches covered in abundant roses and clematis. It makes a wonderful, cool walkway.

below A walled garden filled with a profusion of old-fashioned cottage-garden plants. The narrow path just allows visitors to wander through the flowers, brushing and smelling as they go. The discreet path adds to the sense that this is a secret garden.

right Wide paths created from irregular-sized paving slabs run between square and rectangular beds. The shapes are formal but the planting, by contrast, is exuberant, asymmetrical, and filled with life.

above Beautiful formality is enhanced by the simplicity of this design. Identical beds spread onto a grass pathway with a central stream. The stone edging directs the eye clearly along the straight line while the purple and green add a lively quality.

below The silky heads of this grass, *Hordeum jubatum*, just ask to be caressed as you walk along the central path. They contrast nicely with the cleome beyond, in a more orderly part of the garden.

above A bend in a path adds a note of mystery to any garden scene. Here, a stretch of grass curves away, suggesting a great garden beyond.

left Paths within a path: Here, bold stepping-stones lead in opposite directions while the main grass track forges ahead. Each possibility demands exploration.

edible border

Most of the produce for the kitchen comes from the vegetable and herb gardens, but there is plenty that can be grown in the more ornamental parts of the garden. Many flowers can be eaten or used as a garnish for food, and many vegetables are so decorative that they more than earn their place in borders. Creating a border with culinary as well as decorative value can be very enjoyable and provides great economy of space in a small garden.

PLANTING SCHEME

Atriplex hortensis 'Rubra' (red orach: edible young leaves) (x 60)

Calendula officinalis (calendula: edible flowers) (x 30)

Cynara cardunculus (cardoon: edible blanched stems) (x 6)

Helianthus annuus (sunflower: edible seed) (x 20)

Hemerocallis (daylily: edible opening buds) (x 8)

Although the major concern of this border is decorative, many of the elements are made up from edible plants. Tradition tends to dictate that vegetable and flower gardens are kept separate, but there is no real reason to do so. The unexpected presence of decorative vegetables can give freshness to a planting. The soil preparation, planting, and maintenance for an edible border are just the same as for any other border.

planting scheme

1 *Atriplex hortensis* 'Rubra' (red orach: edible young leaves) (x 60)

2 *Calendula officinalis* (calendula: edible flowers) (x 30)

3 *Cynara cardunculus* (cardoon: edible blanched stems) (x 6)

4 *Helianthus annuus* (sunflower: edible seed) (x 20)

5 *Hemerocallis* (daylily: edible opening buds) (x 8)

edible ornamentals

All the edible plants in this border will enhance a salad while the opening buds of the daylily can be chopped up and stir-fried. These beds are 6 x 20 ft (1.8 x 6 m), but limited space provides even more reason to include edibles.

warning

Not all garden plants are edible. Only those known to be safe should be eaten or used as food decoration.

edible flowering plants and vegetables

The list of plants that are edible in whole or part is very long.
Here are some of the most rewarding, both in terms of their
decorative qualities and for culinary purposes. The less familiar
edible parts of some popular flowers are pointed out.

vegetables

carrots (foliage)

Swiss chard (foliage)

tomatoes (fruit)

peas (flowers and fruit)

corn (foliage)

lettuce (bronze foliage)

flowering plants

Mentha (mint: leaves)

Viola odorata (heartsease:
  flowers)

Tropaeolum majus
  (nasturtium: flowers)

Thymus (thyme: leaves)

Borago officinalis (borage:
  flowers)

Rosa (roses: petals)

Rosmarinus officinalis
  (rosemary: flowers, leaves)

pergola planting

A pergola, whether a substantial wooden structure
or a more refined metal frame, should complement
the pathway borders in shape and plantings.

using a pergola

A pergola straddling the path allows the addition
of several types of vegetables or fruit. The overall
effect is that of an avenue of produce through
which a shady walk can be taken. For a temporary
display, green beans, climbing French beans, or
squash and zucchini can be grown. For a more
permanent display, grapes (right), apples, or pears
can be trained over the arches, or a combination
of apples and pears (above). Keep the climbers
well trained and pruned to get the best from
them. This ensures that sufficient light reaches
the plants below.

care and maintenance

- When you are harvesting only parts of plants,
  take from a different plant each time so that
  there is time for regrowth and to avoid creating
  an unbalanced appearance in the bed.

cottage garden path

The wealth of plants in a traditional cottage garden creates
a wild, romantic air. A riot of colors and shapes speaks of the
informality of a typical country border, which can be created
in any garden if the whole scheme is sympathetic to a freely
planted approach. For those who like an unpredictable display,
this is the perfect path-side look.

PLANTING SCHEME

year-round interest

Juniperus communis 'Depressa
Aurea' (x 1)

spring flowering

Erysimum (x 7)

Forsythia (x 1)

Narcissus (x 19)

Primula vulgaris (x 8)

Tulipa (x 16)

Viola × wittrockiana (x 5)

summer flowering

Achillea ptarmica The Pearl Group (x 3)

Alcea rosea (x 8)

Alchemilla mollis (x 6)

Dianthus 'Mrs Sinkins' (x 6)

Digitalis purpurea (x 5)

Echinops ritro (x 3)

Erigeron 'Serenity' (x 3)

Erodium manescaui (x 1)

Geranium himalayense (x 3)

Hemerocallis fulva (x 3)

Lavandula angustifolia (x 1)

Lychnis coronaria (x 3)

Lysimachia punctata (x 3)

Lysimachia nummularia 'Aurea' (x 3)

Oenothera biennis (x 6)

Papaver somniferum (x 6)

Phlox 'Cherry Pink' (x 6)

Rosa rugosa (x 1)

Stachys byzantina (x 3)

Trollius europaeus (x 1)

Viola cornuta (x 3)

The charm of the original Victorian cottage gardens lay in the fact that they were simply a wonderful collection of plants. With little knowledge of the niceties of garden design, cottage gardeners freely filled gaps in a border and allowed annuals to seed unhindered, creating a busy picture of fruit, vegetables, and native ornamentals.

planning a cottage garden

When laying out a cottage garden, a sense of freedom should be maintained. For an authentic touch, only traditional plants (pre-1900) should be used, although the spirit of a cottage garden will allow any colorful plants to be included providing they do not need too much pampering. Fruit and vegetables should also be included if possible.

practicalities

Besides the useful presence of edible plants, cottage gardens exhibited other practical characteristics. Tight planting prevented weeds from growing, and the use of a wide range of robust plants helped to prevent any one pest or disease from causing wholesale damage.

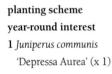

planting scheme
year-round interest

1 *Juniperus communis* 'Depressa Aurea' (x 1)

spring flowering

2 *Erysimum* (x 7)
3 *Forsythia* (x 1)
4 *Narcissus* (x 19)
5 *Primula vulgaris* (x 8)
6 *Tulipa* (x 16)
7 *Viola × wittrockiana* (x 5)

summer flowering

8 *Achillea ptarmica* The Pearl Group (x 3)
9 *Alcea rosea* (x 8)
10 *Alchemilla mollis* (x 6)
11 *Dianthus* 'Mrs Sinkins' (x 6)
12 *Digitalis purpurea* (x 5)
13 *Echinops ritro* (x 3)
14 *Erigeron* 'Serenity' (x 3)
15 *Erodium manescaui* (x 1)
16 *Geranium himalayense* (x 3)
17 *Hemerocallis fulva* (x 3)
18 *Lavandula angustifolia* (x 1)
19 *Lychnis coronaria* (x 3)
20 *Lysimachia punctata* (x 3)
21 *Lysimachia nummularia* 'Aurea' (x 3)
22 *Oenothera biennis* (x 6)
23 *Papaver somniferum* (x 6)
24 *Phlox* 'Cherry Pink' (x 6)
25 *Rosa rugosa* (x 1)
26 *Stachys byzantina* (x 3)
27 *Trollius europaeus* (x 1)
28 *Viola cornuta* (x 3)

maturing time

These pathway borders are 13 x 30 ft (4 x 9 m) and will begin to mature in two years, although the shrubs will take many years to reach their ultimate size.

late-summer and fall interest

The cottage garden should provide interest throughout the year. Although many plants in this border flower for a short period, their foliage is long-lived. Some plants flower repeatedly over a long period or bloom again in fall.

late-season planting

29 *Anemone × hybrida* (x 4)
30 *Aster novae-angliae* 'Andenken an Alma Pötschke' (x 5)
31 *Aster novi-belgii* (x 3)
32 *Buddleja davidii* (x 1)
33 *Crocosmia masoniorum* (x 6)
34 *Helianthus annuus* (x 5)
35 *Sedum spectabile* (x 3)
36 *Solidago* 'Cloth of Gold' (x 4)
37 *Tanacetum vulgare* (x 3)

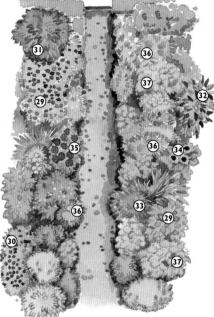

care and maintenance

- Make sure that any tall or flopping plants are well supported. It will be difficult to reach them once the border is in full growth.
- While abundant growth can be very attractive, make sure that paths are not made dangerous by trailing stems.

alternative pathways

As with all garden styles, the appearance of the path can alter the impression made by the cottage garden.

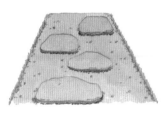

bricks

A simple brick pattern and attractive weathering suit the country style.

grass

Introduce patterns by setting the lawn mower at different heights.

stepping-stones

Stones bedded in beaten earth lead the eye along the path.

scented path

Borders that line paths are always welcome because they bring the viewer close
to the plants. This is doubly rewarding with fragrant borders since the sense
of smell as well as that of sight is stimulated; in many cases, the action
of rubbing against the plants as you pass releases the fragrance.
Lavender and rosemary have very distinctive aromas that pervade
the air for a long distance, far beyond the pathway.

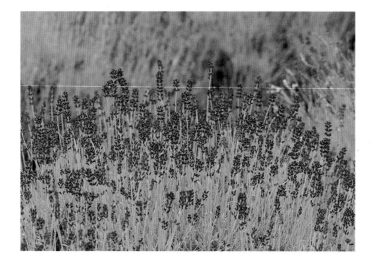

SCENTED PLANTS

fragrant foliage	**fragrant flowers**	
Aloysia triphylla	*Berberis*	*Lupinus*
Artemisia	*Choisya ternata*	*Matthiola*
Lavandula	*Convallaria majalis*	*Nicotiana*
Mentha	*Daphne*	*Osmanthus*
Monarda didyma	*Dianthus*	*Philadelphus*
Myrtus communis	*Erysimum*	*Reseda odorata*
Origanum	*Hesperis matronalis*	*Rhododendron* (azaleas)
Rosmarinus	*Hyacinthus*	*Rosa*
Salvia officinalis	*Iris unguicularis*	*Sarcococca*
	Lathyrus odoratus	*Syringa*
	Lilium	*Viburnum*
		Viola odorata

Fragrant plants should be used more frequently in the garden as they add another special dimension to it. Although some odorous plants are positively offensive, there are many that produce the most wonderful perfumes, such as lavender. These are perfect for creating a relaxing atmosphere, the raison d'être of many a garden today. This delightful path is 9 x 25 ft (2.5 x 7.5 m).

design

It is important that a path is sufficiently wide for its purpose. Most garden paths should be wide enough for two people to walk side by side; an allowance of at least 5 ft (1.5 m) should be made. Paths that are purely for access can be narrower but should still take a wheelbarrow comfortably.

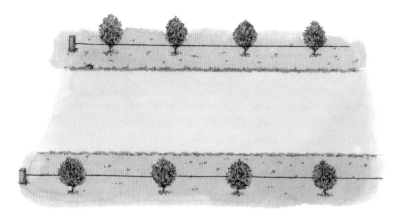

preparing and planting the beds

Using a string as a guide, plant the lavenders in a straight row, each being close enough to the next to merge with its neighbors at maturity, which is about 2 ft (60 cm) all around. To make a consistent picture, use the same variety for all the plants. Seed-grown plants might be cheaper, but the colors can vary. Plant the shrubs to the same depth as they were in their pots, pack down, and water. If possible, mulch the plants to retain moisture and inhibit weeds.

care and maintenance

• Lavender should be pruned in late summer. Remove all flower stems and cut away about 1 in (2.5 cm) of the previous season's growth. Shape the beds into a slightly undulating low hedge (right).

alternative scheme

Cottage-style gardens have paths over which everything seems to spill. Paths for this kind of border should be wide enough to accommodate both the spreading plants and the passage of people. Typical fragrant plants for this type of display are the border pinks, especially the old-fashioned varieties.

alternative planting

1 *Lupinus* 'Kayleigh Ann Savage' (x 1)

2 chives (x 3)

3 *Dianthus* 'Haytor White' (x 1)

4 thyme (x 1)

5 sage (x 1)

6 *Dianthus* 'Gran's Favourite' (x 2)

7 *Artemisia caucasica* (x 1)

8 *Alchemilla mollis* (x 2)

9 *Geranium sanguineum* 'Album' (x 1)

10 mint (x 1)

11 *Dianthus* 'Laced Monarch' (x 1)

12 *Tanacetum parthenium* 'Aureum' (x 1)

raised flower bed

In small paved gardens there seems to be little choice but to grow plants in pots.
However, for a larger display, a generous raised bed is ideal since it holds sufficient
soil to sustain a number of plants, both perennials and seasonal annuals. As well as
permitting more versatile planting layouts, raised beds create different levels,
which add interest to the space. If they border a path, the extra height can be
used to display angular and trailing foliage.

TOOLS AND MATERIALS

broken rocks

concrete

pot shards or coarse gravel

bricks, stones, concrete blocks,

or pressure-treated 4 x 4 in

(100 x 100 mm) or 6 x 6 in

(150 x 150 mm) lumber

landscape fabric

sand

topsoil and well-rotted

organic matter

PLANTING SCHEME

Corylus maxima 'Purpurea' (x 1)

Phormium tenax 'Purpureum' (x 4)

Heuchera micrantha var. *diversifolia* 'Palace Purple' (x 8)

*Please note: This project is more complicated than other projects
in the book. Unless you have previous experience with masonry, it is
best to consult a professional, using these plans as a guide.*

Raised beds are not difficult to create, and they allow great scope for the garden designer, but it is essential to plan and build these structures carefully if they are to fit and work well in a garden. If you live in an area where the ground freezes, you will have to make modifications to ensure the stability of your bed. Consult a local professional for advice.

materials

A variety of materials can be considered for building a raised bed: brick, as here, stone, concrete blocks, and wood. Wood is probably the easiest to use, but make sure it has been pressure-treated. In general, railroad ties are not ideal because they have been impregnated with creosote.

foundations

Brick, stone, and concrete blocks are used in the same way. If the bed is not being built on a solid base, dig out a foundation about 10 in (25 cm) deep. A 4 in (10 cm) layer of broken rocks should be packed into this, topped by a 6 in (15 cm) layer of concrete. The wall is built on top of this.

drainage

It is most important that drainage holes are left in the lower levels of the brickwork to allow excess water to drain (left). A few gaps in the cement can also be sufficient.

finishing details

For brick walls, a line of tiles can be added near the top (right). This detail is not essential, but partly decorative and partly to direct water away from the wall, so that the surface is not stained by repeated drenchings.

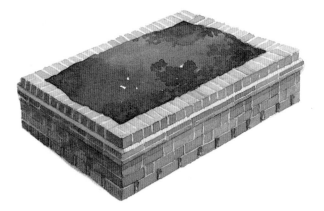

before planting

To aid drainage, add pot shards or coarse gravel to a depth of 3 in (7.5 cm) or more, then a layer of landscape fabric. Fill with good topsoil, plenty of well-rotted organic matter, and some sand to help drainage (left). Pack down as you go. Overfill the bed because the soil will settle with time.

planting scheme

Plant the raised bed with flowering plants according to the scheme shown at right.

planting scheme

1 *Corylus maxima* 'Purpurea' (x 1)
2 *Phormium tenax* 'Purpureum' (x 4)
3 *Heuchera micrantha* var. *diversifolia* 'Palace Purple' (x 8)

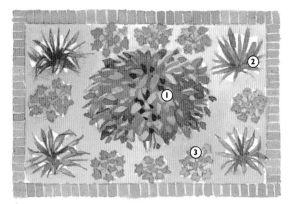

care and maintenance

• Keep the raised bed full of soil and check to make sure the structure is draining efficiently.

alternative materials

Pressure-treated lumber is laid directly onto a flat base. Stagger the lumber at the corners for stability. Leave small gaps for drainage.

Slabs of light brown and gray stone are well suited to cottages and country houses. If the house is made of stone, use the local material.

rose trellis walk

For a garden to be successful it needs to benefit from different heights and contours.
A meandering trellis covered in plants makes a beautiful feature that draws the eye
above the ground and can lead it to a picturesque detail, perhaps a fountain, bench, or
spectacularly planted bed. When the trellis travels the length of a pathway it can also be
enjoyed on a leisurely stroll; add the romance and sweet fragrance of roses and you will
have made a favorite part of any garden.

PLANTING SCHEME

Rosa 'American Pillar' (x 3)
Rosa 'Félicité Perpétue' (x 2)
Geranium 'Johnson's Blue' (x 32)
Rosa 'Constance Spry' (x 2)
Rosa 'L. D. Braithwaite' (x 3)

ALTERNATIVE ROSES

climbers and ramblers

'Albéric Barbier' (yellow and white)
'Alister Stella Gray' (yellow and white)
'Blush Noisette' (pink)
'Cécile Brünner' (pale pink)
'Leverkusen' (lemon yellow)
'Mme Alfred Carrière' (white)
'Maigold' (yellow)
'New Dawn' (pink)
'Paul's Himalayan Musk' (pale pink)
'Paul's Scarlet Climber' (scarlet)
'Sanders' White Rambler' (white)
'Seagull' (white)
'Veilchenblau' (purple)
'Zéphirine Drouhin' (pink)

shrubs

'Charles Austin' (apricot and yellow)
'English Garden' (yellow)
'Gertrude Jekyll' (pink)
'Glamis Castle' (white)
'Graham Thomas' (yellow)
'Heritage' (pink)
'Mary Rose' (pink)
'Othello' (crimson)
'The Countryman' (pink)
'Warwick Castle' (pink)
'Winchester Cathedral' (white)

The trellis is a traditional garden structure that continues to have great appeal. Its versatility and ease of use make it an asset in gardens of any size. The simple, open structure of rustic trellising allows light through while giving support to climbing plants. Always remember the underplanting to give the trellis an abundant, balanced appearance.

a rose walkway

A trellis running the length of a path is an excellent device. It gives structure to a design, and height across the garden, not just at the edges. For a rose walkway, think of repeat-flowering climbing or rambling varieties; these will give a longer season. There is no reason why the roses should be restricted to one type; each section can be different or two roses can be mixed in one section. If the walk is narrow, 'Zéphirine Drouhin,' which is thornless, makes a good choice. This trellis bed is 4 x 25 ft (1.2 x 7.5 m).

erecting a trellis

Make sure the structure is strong because it will have to carry the weight of the roses and also withstand the impact of winds. The posts must be secure in the ground, in holes 2 ft (30 cm) deep, bedded on broken rocks and fixed with concrete (above). For a solid finish, the top beam and diagonals must fit tightly into generous notches at each joint (left), strengthened with nails or screws.

shrub rose border

To complement the trellis, a border of shrub roses can be planted on the other side of the path. The colors should be harmonious with those on the trellis but the bushes should be lower so that other parts of the garden can be seen from the walk. The whole will create a vista of dense roses.

underplanting

The soil can be left bare under both the trellis and the shrub border, but more interest is created if they are underplanted. This will also help to minimize weeds. Keep the planting simple. Do not choose too many different plants, one variety may well be sufficient. These plants should be a finishing touch—the roses are the chief glory.

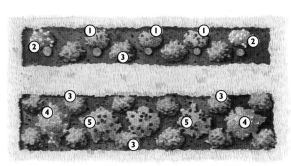

planting scheme
1 *Rosa* 'American Pillar' (x 3)
2 *Rosa* 'Félicité Perpétue' (x 2)
3 *Geranium* 'Johnson's Blue' (x 32)
4 *Rosa* 'Constance Spry' (x 2)
5 *Rosa* 'L. D. Braithwaite' (x 3)

alternative trellising

A very attractive version can be made by linking the tops of the uprights with a thick piece of rope. Additional lengths of rope will give the roses extra support. Tie in the roses as they climb. Look out for and secure any stray stems to prevent accidents.

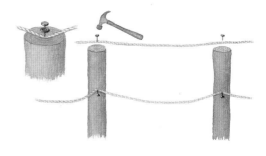

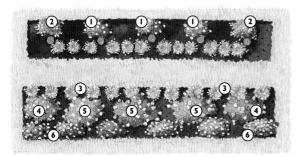

alternative planting

1 *Rosa* 'Mme Alfred Carrière' (x 3)
2 *Rosa* 'Seagull' (x 2)
3 *Dianthus* 'Mrs Sinkins' (numerous)
4 *Rosa* 'Winchester Cathedral' (x 2)
5 *Rosa* 'Glamis Castle' (x 3)
6 *Geranium sanguineum* 'Album' (numerous)

alternative scheme: a white walkway

The perennial favorite is a white scheme. For freshness and purity nothing can match it. If space is limited, white also has an advantage over stronger colors, which can dominate a garden scene. There are scores of beautiful white roses to choose from.

basic techniques

SOIL PREPARATION

The most important aspect of creating a border is thorough preparation. Without it, even the best designs are likely to fail after a year or two, smothered by weeds or starved for nutrients and moisture.

Remove all perennial weeds before planting. Even a small piece of root will reemerge as a weed, by which time it might be difficult to remove without digging up the whole border again. With lighter soils it may be possible to dig the soil and remove any weeds at the same time, but with heavier soils it may be necessary to use a weedkiller; if so, always follow the directions on the package. Dig the soil in the autumn and plant in the spring. This will allow any small piece of weed left in the soil to reveal itself so that it can be removed. In areas with warmer winters it is also possible to dig in spring and plant in fall.

DOUBLE-DIGGING

All borders should be worked but they will be better, especially on heavy soils, if they are double-dug so that the lower portion of earth is also broken up. Do not dig if the soil is too wet. When the border is dug, as much well-rotted organic matter should be incorporated into the soil as possible. This not only improves the structure of the soil but provides nutrients for the plants. Its fibrous nature also helps preserve moisture deep in the soil where the plants' roots need it. Consequently, when double-digging it is important to add generous quantities of organic material to the lower level. Once the soil has been worked, leave it for several months. This will allow the rain and frost to break it down and kill any pests. Residual weeds will also reappear. Avoid walking on the area while it is weathering.

double-digging

1 Dig a trench, 12–18 in (30–45 cm) wide and 12 in (30 cm) deep. Save the removed earth.

2 Work the trench for an additional 12 in (30 cm) and add organic matter. Dig out the next trench and use the earth to fill the first.

3 As before, work through the layer below, breaking up the ground with a fork and adding organic material.

4 When you have reached the end of the border, fill the final trench with the earth removed from the first trench.

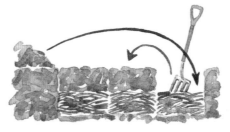

SOIL AMENDMENTS

Chipped or composted bark Best used as a mulch

Composted manure Good all-round amendment as long as it does not contain weed seeds

Garden compost Good all-round amendment as long as it does not contain weed seeds

Leaf mold Excellent amendment and mulch

Peat Little nutrient value and breaks down too quickly to be of great value

Seaweed Excellent amendment, includes plenty of minerals

Spent mushroom compost Good amendment and mulch; includes lime

GARDEN COMPOST

One of the best ways of providing organic material for the garden is to make your own compost. Almost all plant material can be used unless it is too woody or contains weed seeds (woody material can be used once it has been shredded).  Avoid diseased material or virulent weeds. Uncooked vegetable waste from the kitchen is recommended.

Place all the material in a container that has air holes in the sides. Avoid creating too thick a layer of any one material, such as grass cuttings. Keep the bin moist but covered so that the compost retains heat and does not get too wet and chilled in rain. Turn the heap occasionally.

If possible, have two bins: one for collecting new material and one for material that is rotting down; three are even better.

PLANNING

When planning a border, or even a whole garden, there are several basic points to consider before you begin to draw up a plan. The first is to assess what you want to achieve. You may, for example, want a low-maintenance border, or a bright, fun border, or a romantic display in pastel tones; plenty of flowers for cutting might be a priority, or you might prefer a largely foliage effect.

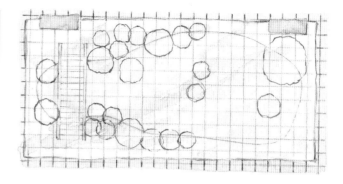

Next, look at where you want to put the border and consider its physical attributes. Does it get plenty of sun or is it in perpetual shade? Is the soil acid or alkaline? Is it wet or dry or just about right? Is it heavy or sandy? All these factors will have a bearing on how much work you will need to put in and on what plants you can and cannot grow. For example, if you live on a chalky soil you will not be able to grow rhododendrons.

After this, decide what plants you want to use to create the desired effect. This is best done over at least one season so that you can go around gardens, notebook in hand, compiling a list of desirable plants. Looking through books also provides plenty of ideas. Having completed your list of plants, it is important to find out whether you can get them locally or if you will have a long search. Adjust your list accordingly.

You are now ready to plot the planting. Using graph paper, draw out the border to scale and then mark out the plants, drawing them at their eventual spread (above). You do not need to be a good draftsman. Adjacent colors should be compatible and the border should have an even spread of interest throughout the year. It is a good idea to draw the bed at different seasons so you can judge the success of the plan, and from the front to compare the plants' relative heights. If problems appear through these sketches, it is so much easier to correct them on paper than after planting.

PLANTING

Before planting, rake or lightly turn over the soil, removing any weeds that have appeared. If only a small amount of organic material was added when the soil was prepared, a light dressing of a granular fertilizer can be raked into the surface. Always follow the directions on the package.

Do not plant in extremes of weather, that is, when it is too hot, wet, or cold. Spring is the most favorable time for planting trees, shrubs, and perennials, although autumn is fine in areas where the winters are mild.

Annuals should not be planted until the threat of frost has passed if they are tender. Plant them in autumn or spring if they are hardy.

Position the plants, still in their pots, on the border to get some idea of how the display will look (below). Make any changes you think are necessary. Dig a hole wider than each plant's rootball and insert the plant so it is at the same depth as it was in its pot or, if it is bare-rooted, in its previous bed. If the roots have become pot-bound or tangled, gently tease them out and spread them in the hole. Fill the hole and pack the soil around the roots.

When planting trees and shrubs, dig a hole much larger than the plant's rootball and work plenty of well-rotted organic material into the bottom of the hole. Also mix some into the soil that will go back into the hole once the plant is in place. If staking the tree or shrub, position the stake before planting in such a way that you will not drive the stake through the roots.

USING A MULCH

Once all the plants are in the bed, water them thoroughly, rake over the surface to level it off, and then apply a mulch. Mulches cover the surface of the soil, helping keep the moisture in, preventing weed seeds from germinating, and preventing the soil surface from hardening, which would restrict the entry of air and moisture. They can also create an attractive background against which to display plants.

There are two types of mulches, organic and inorganic. Organic ones consist of chipped bark, leaf mold, spent mushroom compost, or even grass cuttings and straw.

The last two are unattractive but are valuable in areas that cannot be seen, such as the backs of borders. Inorganic mulches include plastic sheeting (which is ugly and should be covered with soil, gravel, or other stones), gravel, or pebbles. Gravel is good for alpine beds and dry borders.

MAINTENANCE

The best borders are those that are well maintained. Issues such as staking, pruning, and watering must be considered.

staking

Always stake plants that could blow over or become top-heavy in rain. There are many ways to stake perennials. Tall flower spikes can be supported by individual canes; clumps can be held by pea sticks, netting supported between posts, or by commercially available stakes. Stake the plants when they are half-grown; do not wait until they blow over.

Trees and shrubs should be staked with a single or double stake. For most trees it is sufficient to use a single tie low down, 12 in (30 cm) from the ground. For standards and spindly trees use a taller stake and two ties.

twiggy-branch supports

These are versatile, flexible supports that can be drawn together and tied to form a supporting case around vulnerable plants. They can be removed easily.

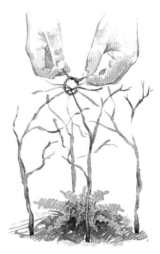

netting support

A net support is a permanent device. The plant grows up and through the mesh which, in time, will be hidden by foliage.

string and stakes
Stakes with a network of strings are useful as a temporary support for larger, spreading shrubs until they are established.

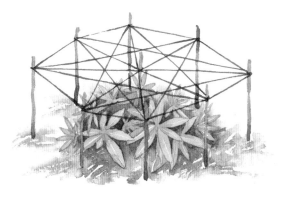

staking trees
A single tie should be placed low down to support a tree. This will give sufficient extra stability until the tree is established.

staking standard bushes
Standards and spindly trees need a taller stake than more robust trees, fitted with two ties (the first tie is shown here, positioned high up the stem).

deadheading
As a general rule, always cut off any dead or dying flowers, unless you want to collect the seeds or save the seed heads for decoration. Many perennials, such as nepeta, a number of geraniums, alchemillas, and oriental poppies, should be cut to the ground after flowering; this will encourage a fresh crop of leaves to grow, making the plant useful for foliage effect.

watering
Water plants in dry conditions, making certain that they get a thorough soaking, the equivalent of at least 1 in (2.5 cm) across the surface. Do not water in full sun. Feeding should

not be necessary if the border is top-dressed regularly. Every autumn, fork in the organic mulch and replace it with a layer of farmyard manure or garden compost. In spring, work this into the border and reapply the usual mulch.

weeding
Remove any weeds on sight. Regular checks will keep weeds under control; if left, they can become difficult and time-consuming to eradicate. With conscientious application it should be possible to hand-weed a border. Chemical herbicides should be avoided on a planted area.

autumn care
In autumn, most perennials should be cut back. This task can be left until spring so that the old stems give the crown some protection from frosts, although tidying during the dormant season means that there is less to do during the spring rush.

pruning
Ornamental trees and evergreen shrubs do not usually need pruning, except to remove any dead or dying branches, although stems can be removed for aesthetic reasons. By contrast, most deciduous shrubs benefit from regular attention. The aim is to keep the bush healthy and vigorous so that it produces good foliage and flowers. To do this, up to one-third of the old wood should be cut off each year, encouraging new growth. As a general rule, the

removing old, dead, and weak wood
A shrub like the one at right should be thoroughly pruned. Dead and weak wood and some of the old stems should go.

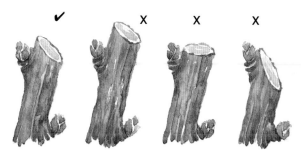

pruning cuts
Correct pruning cuts are very important to the health of plants. Cuts should be sloping, just above a viable bud (above, far left).

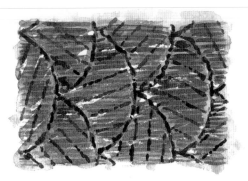

direct sowing: annuals
If clumps of plants are required, mark out the ground with fine sand before sowing.

direct sowing: perennials
1 Dig the soil well, then rake it over to produce a fine tilth for sowing.

2 Make a shallow drill, or furrow, with the edge of a hoe, using guide lines if necessary. Guides can be made using pegs and a length of string.

3 Pour some water into the drill. This will help to consolidate the furrow and ensure that the seeds receive adequate moisture.

4 Sow the seeds, sprinkling a fine line into the shallow trench. Do not overfill as overcrowding can starve seedlings of nourishment.

5 Draw the soil back into the drill with the back of the rake and lightly water.

best time to prune is immediately after the bush has finished flowering. Diseased, dead, or weak growth should also be removed. Pruning cuts should be sloping, just above a viable bud.

SOWING SEED

There are two ways of sowing seeds: directly in the soil and into trays or pots (see illustrations above).

direct sowing

If sowing annuals into a border, break down the dug soil into a fine tilth with a rake. If several clumps of plants are required, mark out each area with some sand so that it is easy to see where to sow. Scatter the seeds over the required area; gently rake them in. Water with a fine-spray watering can. If sowing perennials in a seed bed, draw out a shallow furrow with the edge of a hoe using a guide line if necessary, dampen it, and scatter a sprinkling of seeds along it. Draw the soil back into the drill, then water.

pot sowing

If only a few plants are required or if it is necessary to sow the seeds in gentle heat, they should be sown in a tray or pot. Using a good seed compost, fill the pot and tap it to settle the contents; level and lightly press the compost down. Sow the seeds thinly and cover with a layer of fine grit or compost. Water the compost carefully. Many annuals need to be placed in a warm environment such as a propagating frame or heated greenhouse, but perennials rarely require heat and can be kept outside in a sheltered position. Keep the compost moist until the seeds germinate and then prick out into trays or individual pots. Tender seedlings that have been sheltered should be hardened off in a cold frame before being planted after the threat of frost has passed.

sowing in a pot
Once the seeds have been sprinkled in a pot, cover with compost or a fine grit as recommended for the particular plant.

planting in a tray
Once seedlings have grown in a tray, they should be pricked out carefully and planted on in individual pots to continue growing.

planting bulbs
As a general guide, make sure the planting hole for a bulb is at least three times as deep as the bulb is tall.

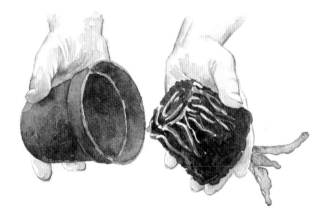

potbound plants
Avoid buying potbound plants such as this.

BULBS

Spring-flowering bulbs are planted in autumn; summer- and autumn-flowering bulbs are planted in spring. As a rule, the depth of the planting hole should be at least three times the height of the bulb. While daffodils, tulips, and several other bulbs can be purchased as dry specimens, it is better to buy many others either "in the green," that is, freshly dug with their leaves still green, or growing in pots. For example, snowdrops should always be purchased in the green, but cyclamens are best bought as potted specimens. Some plants can be relied upon to increase of their own accord. These are often naturalized bulbs, which have been left to grow in grass or under trees. If they become congested, dig them up and replant.

BUYING PLANTS

There are several ways of acquiring plants for a border. The simplest is to buy them. Garden centers sell a reasonably wide range, but specialist nurseries have a much larger selection, including unusual plants. Many nurseries also sell plants by mail order or online, which is a great advantage if they are far from your home. Order early, as demand can outstrip supply for many catalog plants. Inform the nursery if you expect to be away when the order is sent, otherwise you might come home to a box of dead plants. When buying plants, do not always go for the largest specimen. A medium-sized plant, free from pests and diseases, is best. Do not buy pot-bound plants (above).

The alternative to buying plants is to grow them from seeds, by division, or from cuttings. This is a much cheaper approach, but plants will need time to mature. Rare plants are often available only as seeds.

useful addresses

NURSERIES AND PLANT SPECIALISTS

Avant Gardens
710 High Hill Road
North Dartmouth
MA 02747-1363
(508) 998-8819
www.avantgardensne.com
Uncommon plants, including
annuals and tender perennials,
hardy perennials, alpines, and
woody plants. Plenty of plants
for container gardening.

Bamboo Sourcery
666 Wagnon Road
Sebastapol, CA 95472
(707) 823-5866
www.bamboosourcery.com
Bamboo, from *Arundinaria*
to *Yushania*.

Bluestone Perennials
7211 Middle Ridge Road
Madison, OH 44057-3096
(800) 852-5243
www.bluestoneperennials.com
Perennials, plants, herbs,
ornamental shrubs, and bulbs.

The Cook's Garden
P.O. Box 1889
Southampton, PA 18966
(800) 457-9703
www.cooksgarden.com
An inspiring collection of
seeds for herbs, vegetables,
and flowers.

Dutch Gardens
144 Intervale Road
Burlington, VT 05401
(800) 944-2250
www.dutchgardens.com
Holland's finest bulbs.

Eastern Plant Specialties
P.O. Box 5692
Clark, NJ 07066
(732) 382-2508
www.easternplant.com
Special emphasis on native
and woodland plants.

Glasshouse Works
P.O. Box 97
Church Street
Stewart, OH 45778-0097
(800) 837-2142
www.rareplants.com
A good source for tropicals,
perennials, herbs, and annuals.
Coleus is a specialty.

Heronswood Nursery
7530 NE 288th Street
Kingston, WA 98346
(360) 297-4172
www.heronswood.com
An exquisite collection for
collectors and connoisseurs:
perennials, annuals, herbs,
trees, and shrubs.

Johnny's Selected Seeds
955 Benton Avenue
Winslow, ME 04901
(207) 861-3900
www.johnnyseeds.com
All the basics, plus many
unusual varieties.

Lilypons Water Gardens
6800 Lilypons Road
P.O. Box 10
Buckeystown, MD 21717
www.lilypons.com
Water-gardening supplies, as
well as tropical lilies and lotus.

McClure & Zimmerman
108 W. Winnebago Street
P.O. Box 368
Friesland, WI 53935-0368
(800) 883-6998
www.mzbulb.com
Not just autumn bulbs,
but many of the summer
bloomers, including
flowering onions.

Miller Nurseries
5060 West Lake Road
Canandaigua, NY 14424
(800) 836-9630
www.millernurseries.com
Grape specialists, but also
plenty of other fruit trees
and shrubs.

New England Bamboo Co.
5 Granite Street
Rockport, MA 01966
(978) 546-3581
www.newengbamboo.com
Bamboo, of course, but also
a wonderful selection of
ornamental grasses.

Plant Delights Nursery
9241 Sauls Road
Raleigh, NC 27603
(919) 772-4794
www.plantdelights.com
An amazing selection of
hostas. Plus cannas, callas,
and other tropicals. Also
bog and aquatic plants.

Select Seeds
180 Stickney Hill Road
Union, CT 06076
(800) 684-0395
www.selectseeds.com
The focus here is on heirloom
seeds, but plants are offered,
too: herbs, annuals, perennials.

Stokes
P.O. Box 548
Buffalo, NY 14240
(800) 396-9238
www.stokeseeds.com
Vegetables, seeds, flowers,
annuals, perennials, herbs,
and some bulbs.

The Thyme Garden
20546 Alsea Highway
Alsea, OR 97324
(541) 487-8671
www.thymegarden.com
Sixty varieties of thyme;
hundreds of other plants,
including a good selection
of lavenders.

Waterford Gardens
74 East Allendale Road
Saddle River, NJ 07458
(201) 327-0721
www.waterfordgardens.com
Pond supplies, plants, and fish.

Wayside Gardens
1 Garden Lane
Hodges, SC 29695-0001
(800) 213-0379
www.waysidegardens.com
Plants, perennials, and flowers.

We-Du Natives
2055 Polly Spout Road
Marion, NC 28752
(828) 738-8300
www.we-du.com
Perennials, wildflowers,
flowers, shrubs, trees, bulbs,
aquatic plants, and ferns.

White Flower Farm
P.O. Box 50
Litchfield, CT 06759
(800) 503-9624
www.whiteflowerfarm.com
Perennials, annuals, and
some shrubs.

PLANTERS AND GARDEN STRUCTURES

**Adkins Architectural
Antiques**
3515 Fannin Street
Houston, TX 77004
(800) 522-6547
www.adkinsantiques.com
Gargoyles and griffins, and
other grand garden ornaments.

Charleston Gardens
650 Queen Street
Charleston, SC 29403
(800) 469-0118
www.charlestongardens.com
Planters and jardinieres;
lighting, garden features,
and fountains.

Florentine Craftsmen
46–24 28th Street
Long Island City, NY 11101
(718) 937-7632
www.florentinecraftsmen.com
Classic furniture, fountains,
statuary, planters, and urns.

Gardener's Supply Company
128 Intervale Road
Burlington, VT 05401
(888) 833-1412
www.gardeners.com
Lightweight planters, as well
as obelisks, willow fences and
borders, trellises, and statuary.

Kinsman Company
P.O. Box 428
Pipersville, PA 18947
(800) 733-4146
www.kinsmangarden.com
Moss-lined baskets, topiary
forms, hooks, and wreath rings.

**Martha Stewart Catalog
for Living**
(800) 950-7130
www.marthastewart.com
Classy containers and
ornaments.

Plow & Hearth
P.O. Box 6000
Madison, VA 22727
(800) 494-7544
www.plowhearth.com
Furniture, cushions, all-
weather wicker, outdoor
fireplaces, and lanterns.

Pottery Barn
Stores nationwide
(888) 779-5176
www.potterybarn.com
Tables, chairs, and a variety
of garden ornamentation.

Seibert & Rice
P.O. Box 365
Short Hills, NJ 07078
(973) 467-8266
www.seibert-rice.com
Exquisite terra cotta, pots,
troughs, and urns.

Smith & Hawken
P.O. Box 8690
Pueblo, CO 81008
(800) 940-1170
www.smithandhawken.com
Simple and classic containers.

Stone Forest
P.O. Box 2840
Santa Fe, NM 87504
(888) 682-2987
www.stoneforest.com
Hand-carved granite
sculpture in Japanese and
contemporary styles. Also
basins, fountains, functional
sculpture, stepping stones.

Target Stores
Stores nationwide
(888) 304-4000
www.target.com
Reasonably priced outdoor
furniture—with a little flair.

Trellis Structures
60 River Street
Beverly, MA 01915
(888) 285-4624
www.trellisstructures.com
Arbors and trellises from
traditional to contemporary;
pergolas, chairs, and benches.

Vermont Outdoor Furniture
9 Auburn Street
Barre, VT 05641
(800) 588-8834
www.vermontoutdoor
  furniture.com
Simple, beautiful wooden
benches, chairs, porch swings,
gliders, and tables.

Walt Nicke's Garden Talk
P.O. Box 433
Topsfield, MA 01983
(978) 887-3388
www.gardentalk.com
Arches, obelisks and gazebos,
as well as fine tools and garden
ornaments.

Wood Classic
47 Steves Lane
Gardiner, NY 12525
(845) 255-7871
Elegant, simple wood
furniture: chairs, benches,
gliders, umbrellas, and tables.

LUMBER AND BUILDING SUPPLIES

Ace Hardware Corporation
Stores nationwide
(630) 990-6600
www.acehardware.com

The Home Depot
Stores nationwide
(800) 430-3376
www.homedepot.com
Bricks, pavers, stone,
lumber, and hardware.

plant index

Page numbers in *italic* refer to the illustrations

A

Acaena (Z6–9) 46
  A. saccaticupula 'Blue Haze'
    (Z6–9) 62–5
Achillea clavennae (Z3) 47
  A. filipendulina 'Gold Plate'
    (Z3–9) 10–13
  A. millefolium 'Cerise Queen'
    (Z3–8) 10–13
  A. ptarmica The Pearl Group
    (Z4–9) 17, 80–3
Agapanthus 'Ben Hope'
    (Z8–10) 54–7
  A. 'Bressingham Blue'
    (Z8–10) 13, 65
Agave (Z9–11) 49
Alcea rosea (Z2–10) 80–3
  A. rugosa (Z2–10) 14–17
Alchemilla (Z3–8) 99
  A. alpina (Z3–8) 44–7
  A. conjuncta (Z3–8) 44–7
  A. mollis (Z3–7) 10–13,
    58–61, 69, 80–3, 87
Allium (Z1–9) 9, 72
  A. cristophii (Z9) 30–3, 36–9
  A. hollandicum (Z8) 30–3
  A. h. 'Purple Sensation' (Z8)
    54–7
  A. schoenoprasum (chives)
    (Z5) 8, 43, 87
  A. unifolium (Z8) 62–5
Aloysia triphylla (Z8) 84
Alternanthera 'Aurea Nana'
    (Z8) 18–21
  A. 'Brilliantissima' (Z8)
    18–21
  A. 'Versicolor' (Z8) 18–21
Althaea officinalis 'Romney
    Marsh' (Z3) 62–5
Anaphalis margaritacea (Z4–8)
    17
Androsace carnea subsp. laggeri
    (Z5–8) 47
Anemone hupehensis var.
    japonica 'Prinz Heinrich'
    (Z5–8) 14–17

A. × hybrida (Z5–8) 83
  A. × h. 'Honorine Jobert'
    (Z5–8) 17
  A. nemorosa (Z5–8) 61, 68
Anthemis (Z4–9) 72
  A. tinctoria (Z4–8) 30–3
Antirrhinum (Z7) 42
  A. majus 'His Excellency'
    (Z7) 14–17
  A. 'White Wonder' (Z7) 17
  A. 'Yellow Triumph' (Z7) 13
apples 79
Aquilegia (columbine) (Z3–9) 9
  A. 'Crimson Star' (Z3–9)
    10–13
  A. flabellata (Z3–9) 33
Argyranthemum 'Jamaica
    Primrose' (Z9) 13
Armeria juniperifolia (Z4–8) 47
Artemisia (Z3–9) 84
  A. alba 'Canescens' (Z5–9)
    36–9
  A. caucasica (Z5–7) 87
  A. 'Powis Castle' (Z5–8) 17,
    25, 54–7
Arum italicum (Z6–9) 68
Aruncus dioicus (Z3–9) 26–9,
    68
Asphodeline lutea (Z6–8)
    10–13, 30–3, 54–7
Aster alpinus (Z4–9) 47
  A. ericoides 'Blue Star' (Z5–8)
    13
  A. × frikartii (Z5–8) 33
  A. × f. 'Mönch' (Z5–8) 13
  A. novae-angliae 'Andenken
    an Alma Pötschke' (Z5–8)
    14–17, 83
  A. novi-belgii (Z4–8) 83
  A. n.-b. 'Carnival' (Z4–8)
    14–17
Astilbe (Z3–9) 68
  A. × arendsii 'Fanal' (Z4–9)
    14–17
  A. chinensis var. pumila
    (Z3–8) 10–13
Atriplex hortensis var. rubra
    (red orach) (annual) 14–17,
    30–3, 76–9

Aubrieta 'Joy' (Z4–9) 47
azaleas see Rhododendron

B

Ballota pseudodictamnus
    (Z7–9) 62–5
Baptisia australis (Z4–9) 13,
    26–9
beets 43
Begonia (Z10) 42
  B. × carrierei 'Red Ascot'
    (Z10) 40–3
Berberis (Z5–8) 84
Bergenia 'Silberlicht' (Z4–8)
    58–61
bok-choy 43
Borago officinalis (borage)
    (annual) 79
boxwood see Buxus
Brunnera macrophylla (Z3–9)
    58–61
Brussels sprouts 43
Buddleja davidii (Z5–9) 83
Bupleurum falcatum (Z3) 13
Buxus (boxwood) (Z5–8) 38,
    42
  B. sempervirens 'Suffruticosa'
    (Z6–8) 40–3

C

cabbages 43
Calendula officinalis (Z6) 76–7
Callistemon citrinus (Z8) 65
Camellia japonica (Z7–9) 69
Campanula carpatica (Z4–8)
    47
  C. lactiflora (Z4–8) 13
  C. latifolia (Z4–8) 58–61
  C. persicifolia (Z4–8) 26–9
  C. portenschlagiana (Z4–8)
    13
Canna 'Orange Perfection'
    (Z8–10) 33
Cardiocrinum giganteum (Z7)
    68
cardoon see Cynara
    cardunculus
Carex pendula (Z5–9) 66–9
carrots 43, 79

Centranthus ruber (Z4–9)
    14–17
Chamaecyparis lawsoniana
    'Pembury Blue' (Z5–8)
    62–5
chives see Allium
    schoenoprasum
Choisya ternata (Z7–9) 84
Cistus × fernandesiae 'Anne
    Palmer' (Z7–9) 62–5
  C. × skanbergii (Z7–9) 62–5
Clematis (Z7–9) 74
  C. 'Marie Boisselot' (Z5–8)
    17
Cleome (annual) 75
columbine see Aquilegia
Convallaria majalis (Z2–9) 61,
    68, 84
Convolvulus althaeoides (Z8)
    47
Cordyline australis (Z10)
    18–21, 65
corn 79
Cornus canadensis (Z2–7) 68
  C. controversa 'Variegata'
    (Z5) 22–5
Corydalis flexuosa (Z5–8) 68
Corylus avellana (Z4–8) 58–61
  C. maxima 'Purpurea' (Z5–9)
    88–91
Cosmos 'Purity' (annual) 17
Cotyledon orbiculata (Z8) 57
Crinum × powellii (Z6) 14–17
Crocosmia × crocosmiiflora
    'Emily McKenzie' (Z5) 33
  C. × c. 'Solfaterre' (Z5) 22–5
  C. masoniorum (Z6) 83
Cyclamen (Z6–9) 48, 101
  C. coum (Z6) 61, 68
  C. hederifolium (Z6) 69
Cynara cardunculus (cardoon)
    (Z6) 30–3, 76–9

D

daffodils see Narcissus
Dahlia 'Betty Bowen' (Z9)
    14–17
  D. 'Bishop of Llandaff'
    (Z7–9) 33

Daphne (Z4–8) 84
  D. tangutica (Z6–7) 47
daylily see *Hemerocallis*
Delphinium (Z3–8) 13, 33
  D. 'Fenella' (Z3–7) 26–9
Deschampsia flexuosa (Z5) 44–7
Deutzia × *elegantissima* (Z5–8) 14–17
Dianthus (pinks) (Z4–8) 84, 87
  D. 'Annabel' (Z4–8) 47
  D. chinensis 'Firecarpet' (Z4–8) 14–17
  D. 'Doris' (Z4–8) 26–9
  D. 'Gran's Favourite' (Z4–8) 87
  D. 'Haytor White' (Z4–8) 17, 87
  D. 'Inchmery' (Z4–8) 25
  D. 'Laced Monarch' (Z4–8) 87
  D. 'Little Jock' (Z4–8) 47
  D. 'Mrs Sinkins' (Z4–8) 80–3, 95
Diascia (Z7–9) 42, 72
Dicentra 'Bountiful' (Z3–8) 58–61
Digitalis (foxgloves) (Z3–8) 9
  D. purpurea (Z3–8) 58–61, 80–3
  D. p. 'Alba' (Z3–8) 17
Dorotheanthus bellidiformis (annual) 57
Dryopteris filix-mas (Z2) 66–9
Dudleya farinosa (Z8) 18–21

E
Echeveria elegans (Z8) 18–21
  E. pulvinata (Z8) 18–21
  E. secunda var. *glauca* (Z8) 18–21
Echinacea purpurea (Z3–9) 14–17
Echinops ritro (Z4–8) 13, 80–3
Epilobium angustifolium 'Album' (Z2–8) 17
Epimedium × *rubrum* (Z4–8) 58–61
  E. × *versicolor* 'Sulphureum' (Z5–8) 69
Eranthis hyemalis (Z5) 61, 68
Eremurus subsp. *stenophyllus* (Z5–8) 10–13
Erigeron (Z2–9) 46

E. 'Serenity' (Z2–9) 80–3
Erinus alpinus (Z4–7) 47
Erodium corsicum (Z5–8) 47
  E. manescaui (Z5–8) 80–3
Eryngium alpinum (Z5–8) 13
  E. giganteum (Z4–8) 54–7, 65
  E. × *tripartitum* (Z5–8) 33
Erysimum (Z5–9) 80–3, 84
Euphorbia amygdaloides (Z5–9) 68
  E. a. var. *robbiae* (Z7) 58–61, 69
  E. characias (Z7) 62–5
  E. c. subsp. *wulfenii* (Z7–9) 22–5, 65, 66–9
  E. dulcis 'Chameleon' (Z6) 22–5, 54–7
  E. griffithii 'Fireglow' (Z5–9) 10–13, 33
  E. × *martinii* (Z7) 30–3
  E. myrsinites (Z7) 47
  E. stricta (Z6) 44–7
Exochorda × *macrantha* 'The Bride' (Z5–8) 17

F
Ferula communis (Z6–9) 22–5
Filipendula rubra (Z4–8) 14–17
Foeniculum vulgare (Z4–9) 66–9
Forsythia (Z5–9) 80–3
Fragaria (Z5) 72
French beans 79

G
Galanthus nivalis (snowdrops) (Z4–7) 60, 61, 68, 101
Garrya elliptica (Z8) 69
Gentiana septemfida (Z2–8) 47
Geranium (Z3–9) 72, 99
  G. 'Ann Folkard' (Z5–8) 14–17
  G. cinereum subsp. *subcaulescens* (Z4–9) 47
  G. himalayense (Z4–8) 80–3
  G. 'Johnson's Blue' (Z4–9) 13, 92–5
  G. macrorrhizum (Z3–8) 22–5, 69
  G. × *magnificum* (Z4–8) 22–5, 58–61
  G. nodosum (Z6) 66–9
  G. palmatum (Z9) 22–5, 70–3
  G. pratense (Z4–8) 58–61

G. p. 'Mrs Kendall Clark' (Z4–8) 44–7
  G. psilostemon (Z4–8) 14–17
  G. × *riversleaianum* 'Mavis Simpson' (Z4–8) 26–9
  G. sanguineum 'Album' (Z4–8) 87, 95
Geum 'Borisii' (Z4–8) 33
grapes 79
grasses 24, 32, 49, 65
green beans 79
Gypsophila paniculata 'Bristol Fairy' (Z4–8) 17

H
heartsease see *Viola odorata*
Hedera (ivy) (Z6–10) 68
Helenium autumnale (Z3) 10–13
Helianthemum 'Annabel' (Z6–8) 47
Helianthus annuus (sunflower) (annual) 76–9, 83
  H. 'Lemon Queen' (Z3–9) 30–3
  H. 'Loddon Gold' (Z3–9) 10–13
Heliotropium arborescens 'P. K. Lowther' (Z9) 39
hellebores 48
Helleborus foetidus (Z4–9) 58–61
  H. orientalis (Z5–9) 68
Hemerocallis (daylily) (Z3–9) 76–9
  H. fulva (Z3–9) 80–3
  H. 'Marion Vaughn' (Z3–9) 10–13
  H. 'Pink Damask' (Z3–9) 66–9
hepaticas 48
Hesperis matronalis (Z4–9) 84
Heuchera micrantha var. *diversifolia* 'Palace Purple' (Z4–8) 22–5, 88–91
  H. sanguinea (Z4–8) 30–3
honeysuckle see *Lonicera*
Hordeum jubatum (Z5) 75
Hosta (Z3–9) 24
  H. fortunei var. *aureomarginata* (Z3–9) 66–9
  H. lancifolia (Z3–9) 22–5
  H. sieboldiana var. *elegans* (Z3–9) 50–3

H. Tardiana Group 'Halcyon' (Z3–9) 22–5, 58–61, 66–9
  H. tokudama f. *flavocircinalis* (Z3–9) 50–3
Houttuynia cordata (Z5–7) 68
Hyacinthoides hispanica (Z5) 69
  H. non-scripta (Z5) 61, 66–9
Hyacinthus (Z6) 84
Hydrocharis morsus-ranae (Z4) 50–3
Hypericum olympicum 'Citrinum' (Z6) 47

I
Impatiens (Z9) 42
Iris ensata (Z4–9) 48
  I. foetidissima (Z6–9) 68
  I. pseudacorus 'Variegata' (Z5–9) 50–3
  I. sibirica (Z4–9) 22–5, 50–3, 58–61
  I. unguicularis (Z6–9) 84

J
Jovibarba hirta (Z5–8) 57
Juniperus communis 'Compressa' (Z3–8) 47
  J. c. 'Depressa Aurea' (Z3–8) 80–3
  J. scopulorum 'Skyrocket' (Z3–8) 54–7

K
Kirengeshoma palmata (Z5–8) 68
Kniphofia 'Painted Lady' (Z6–9) 22–5
  K. 'Percy's Pride' (Z6–9) 10–13
  K. 'Yellow Hammer' (Z6–9) 13, 30–3

L
Lamium galeobdolon (Z3–9) 66–9
  L. maculatum 'White Nancy' (Z3–9) 17
Lathyrus odoratus (annual) 84
  L. vernus (Z4) 68
Lavandula (lavender) (Z5) 42, 84, 86–7
  L. angustifolia (Z5) 80–3
  L. officinalis (Z5) 62–5

lavender *see Lavandula*
leeks *43*
lettuce *43*, *79*
Lewisia tweedyi (Z5–8) *47*
Leymus arenarius (Z6–9) *26–9*
Ligustrum lucidum 'Aureum'
    (Z7) *30–3*
Lilium (Z4–8) *48*, *84*
    L. 'Limelight' (Z6) *13*
    L. martagon (Z4) *66–9*, *68*
    L. regale (Z5) *26–9*
Linaria purpurea 'Springside
    White' (Z4–9) *62–5*
Lobelia (Z9) *42*
    L. × gerardii 'Vedrariensis'
    (Z2–9) *30–3*
Lonicera (honeysuckle) (Z2–9)
    8
Lupinus (lupine) (Z4–8) *84*
    L. arboreus (Z7–9) *30–3*
    L. 'The Chatelaine' (Z4–8)
    14–17
    L. 'Kayleigh Ann Savage'
    (Z4–8) *87*
Lychnis chalcedonica (Z4–8)
    10–13
    L. coronaria (Z4–8) *62–5*,
    80–3
    L. viscaria 'Flore Pleno'
    (Z3–9) *14–17*
Lysichiton americanus (Z5–9)
    22–5
Lysimachia ciliata 'Firecracker'
    (Z4–9) *22–5*
    L. nummularia 'Aurea' (Z4–9)
    80–3
    L. punctata (Z4–9) *80–3*
Lythrum virgatum 'The Rocket'
    (Z3–9) *14–17*

M
Macleaya cordata (Z3) *22–5*
Malva moschata (Z5–9) *10–13*
Matthiola (Z6) *84*
Meconopsis betonicifolia
    (Z6–8) *68*
    M. cambrica (Z6–8) *22–5*
Mentha (mint) (Z5–9) *46*, *79*,
    84, *87*
Milium effusum (Z5–8) *36–9*
Mimulus guttatus (Z6–9) *44–7*
    M. luteus (Z6) *50–3*
    M. 'Royal Velvet' (Z6) *10–13*
mint *see Mentha*

Miscanthus sinensis (Z5–9) *13*,
    22–5, *65*
Monarda didyma (Z4–9) *84*
mullein *see Verbascum*
Myosotis (forget–me–nots)
    (Z4–9) *13*
    M. sylvatica (Z4–9) *58–61*
Myrtus communis (Z8) *84*

N
Narcissus (daffodils) (Z4–8)
    33, *80–3*, *101*
    N. pseudonarcissus (Z9–11)
    61
nasturtium *see Tropaeolum
    majus*
Nectaroscordum siculum (Z6)
    10–13, *62–5*, *66–9*
Nepeta (Z4–9) *99*
    N. × faassenii (Z4–9) *25*
    N. racemosa (Z4) *66–9*
Nerine bowdenii (Z8) *25*
Nicotiana (Z7–8) *84*
    N. langsdorffii (Z8) *40–3*
    N. sylvestris (Z8) *17*
Nigella damascena (annual) *13*
Nymphaea 'René Gérard' (Z6)
    50–3

O
Oenothera biennis (Z4) *80–3*
    O. fruticosa 'Fyreverken'
    (Z4–8) *10–13*
    O. stricta (Z5) *10–13*, *30–3*
Omphalodes cappadocica
    (Z5–8) *68*
    O. linifolia (annual) *17*
    O. verna (Z6) *68*
onions *43*
Onopordum acanthium (Z6)
    62–5
Ophiopogon planiscapus
    'Nigrescens' (Z6–9) *65*
Origanum (Z4–9) *84*
Osmanthus (Z6–9) *84*
Oxalis acetosella (Z3) *68*

P
Pachysandra terminalis (Z6) *68*
pansies *13*; *see also Viola*
Papaver (poppies) (Z2–9) *99*
    P. atlanticum (Z6–8) *33*
    P. orientale 'Mrs Perry' (Z3–7)
    26–9

P. somniferum (annual)
    14–17, *26–9*, *62–5*, *80–3*
parsley *43*
pears *79*
peas *79*
Pennisetum villosum (Z7–9)
    54–7
Penstemon 'Andenken an
    Friedrich Hahn' (Z6–9)
    10–13, *14–17*
    P. 'Evelyn' (Z6–9) *14–17*
    P. heterophyllus (Z6–9) *54–7*
Perovskia atriplicifolia (Z6) *13*
Persicaria (Z3–9) *72*
    P. affinis (Z3–8) *14–17*, *54–7*,
    58–61
Phalaris arundinacea (Z4–9)
    50–3
Philadelphus (Z5–9) *84*
Phlox (Z4–9) *9*
    P. 'Cherry Pink' (Z4–8) *80–3*
    P. douglasii 'Crackerjack'
    (Z4–9) *47*
    P. paniculata 'Fujiyama'
    (Z4–8) *17*
Phormium tenax (Z8–10) *54–7*
    P. t. 'Purpureum' (Z8–10)
    88–91
Physostegia virginiana 'Red
    Beauty' (Z3–9) *14–17*
Phytolacca americana (Z3–9)
    22–5
Picea mariana 'Nana' (Z2) *47*
pincushion flower *see Scabiosa*
pinks *see Dianthus*
pole beans *43*
Polemonium pauciflorum (Z7)
    10–13
Polygala chamaebuxus var.
    grandiflora (Z5–7) *47*
Polygonatum × hybridum
    (Z4–8) *17*, *68*
Polystichum setiferum (Z7)
    22–5
poppies *see Papaver*
Primula (Z4–10) *48*, *68*
    P. 'Blue Riband' (Z5–8) *26–9*
    P. pulverulenta (Z5–8) *50–3*
    P. vulgaris (Z5–8) *80–3*
Pulmonaria (Z4–9) *72*
    P. officinalis (Z4–8) *58–61*
    P. o. 'Sissinghurst White'
    (Z4–8) *17*
Pulsatilla vulgaris (Z4–9) *47*

Pyrus salicifolia 'Pendula'
    (Z5–7) *25*, *26–9*

R
radishes *43*
Ranunculus lingua (Z4) *50–3*
red orach *see Atriplex hortensis
    * var. *rubra*
Reseda odorata (annual) *84*
Rhodiola rosea (Z4–8) *57*
Rhododendron (Z5–10) *84*, *97*
Rhodohypoxis baurii (Z8) *47*
Rodgersia podophylla (Z5–7)
    22–5
Romneya coulteri (Z6–9) *22–5*
Rosa (roses) (Z2–8) *8*, *35*, *74*,
    79, *84*
    R. 'Albéric Barbier' (Z7) *92*
    R. 'Alister Stella Gray' (Z7)
    73, *92*
    R. 'American Pillar' (Z7) *92–5*
    R. 'Ballerina' (Z7) *36–9*
    R. 'Blush Noisette' (Z7) *92*
    R. 'Cécile Brünner' (Z7) *92*
    R. 'Charles Austin' (Z7) *70*,
    72, *92*
    R. 'Constance Spry' (Z7) *70*,
    72, *92–5*
    R. 'Cottage Rose' (Z7) *70*, *72*
    R. 'The Countryman' (Z7)
    70, *92*
    R. 'Dark Lady' (Z7) *70*
    R. 'English Garden' (Z7) *70*,
    92
    R. 'Félicité Perpétue' (Z7)
    92–5
    R. 'Frau Karl Druschki' (Z7)
    9
    R. gallica var. *officinalis*
    'Versicolor' (Z5) *26–9*
    R. 'Gertrude Jekyll' (Z7) *70*,
    92
    R. 'Glamis Castle' (Z7) *70*,
    92, *95*
    R. glauca (Z2) *30–3*
    R. 'Golden Celebration' (Z7)
    70, *72*
    R. 'Graham Thomas' (Z7) *9*,
    70, *73*, *92*
    R. 'Heritage' (Z7) *70*, *72*, *92*
    R. 'Iceberg' (Z7) *17*
    R. 'L. D. Braithwaite' (Z7)
    70, *92–5*
    R. 'Leverkusen' (Z7) *92*

R. 'Mme Alfred Carrière'
(Z7) 92, 95
R. 'Mme Isaac Pereire' (Z7)
14–17
R. 'Maigold' (Z7) 92
R. 'Mary Rose' (Z7) 70, 92
R. 'New Dawn' (Z7) 69, 92
R. 'Othello' (Z7) 70, 92
R. 'Paul's Himalayan Musk'
(Z7) 92
R. 'Paul's Scarlet Climber'
(Z7) 92
R. 'Pink Grootendorst' (Z7)
70–3
R. 'Ramona' (Z7) 58–61
R. rugosa (Z2) 80–3
R. 'Sanders' White Rambler'
(Z7) 92
R. 'Seagull' (Z7) 92, 95
R. 'Veilchenblau' (Z7) 92
R. 'Warwick Castle' (Z7) 70,
92
R. 'Wife of Bath' (Z7) 70
R. 'Winchester Cathedral'
(Z7) 70, 72, 92, 95
R. 'Zéphirine Drouhin' (Z7)
92, 94
Rosmarinus (rosemary)
(Z6–10) 84
R. officinalis (Z6–10) 79

S
sage 87
Salix babylonica (Z6–8) 50–3
Salvia (Z5–10) 8, 42
S. forsskaolii (Z7) 26–9
S. fulgens (Z9) 39
S. greggii (Z7) 70–3
S. jurisicii (Z6) 62–5
S. officinalis (Z5) 84
S. o. 'Purpurascens' (Z5) 62–5
S. patens (Z8) 39
S. sclarea (Z5) 26–9
S. s. var. turkestanica (Z5) 13
S. × superba 'Superba' (Z5)
62–5
S. × sylvestris 'Blauhügel'
(Z5) 13
S. uliginosa (Z5) 13
Sanguisorba obtusa (Z5–8)
14–17
Santolina (Z7) 42
Sarcococca (Z6–9) 84

Scabiosa (pincushion flower)
(Z4–9) 8
S. caucasica 'Clive Greaves'
(Z4–9) 36–9
Schizostylis coccinea (Z6)
14–17
Sedum acre (Z3–9) 18–21, 57
S. aizoon 'Euphorbioides'
(Z4–9) 57
S. 'Bertram Anderson' (Z3–8)
57
S. 'Herbstfreude' (Z3–9)
40–3, 57, 62–5
S. lydium (Z3–9) 57
S. 'Morchen' (Z4–9) 57
S. 'Ruby Glow' (Z5–9) 10–13,
57
S. spathulifolium 'Aureum'
(Z5–7) 57
S. spectabile (Z4–9) 14–17, 83
S. s. 'Meteor' (Z4–9) 57
S. spurium 'Schorbuser Blut'
(Z3–9) 57
S. 'Sunset Cloud' (Z4–9) 57
S. telephium subsp. maximum
'Atropurpureum' (Z4–9)
14–17, 54–7
S. 'Vera Jameson' (Z4–9) 54–7
Sempervivum 'Commander
Hay' (Z4–8) 57
S. 'Glowing Embers' (Z4–8)
57
S. 'Lady Kelly' (Z4–8) 57
S. tectorum (Z4–8) 57
Silene dioica (Z6) 26–9
Silybum marianum (Z6) 22–5
Sisyrinchium idahoense subsp.
bellum (Z8) 47

S. striatum (Z6–9) 26–9
Smilacina racemosa (Z4–9) 17,
68
Smyrnium perfoliatum (Z9)
66–9
snowdrops see Galanthus
nivalis
Solidago 'Cloth of Gold'
(Z4–9) 83
S. cutleri (Z4–9) 10–13
S. 'Laurin' (Z4–9) 10–13
snapdragon see Antirrhinum
squashes 79
Stachys (Z4–9) 72
S. byzantina (Z4–8) 17, 25,
39, 54–7, 62–5, 80–3
Stipa gigantea (Z7–9) 54–7
Stylophorum diphyllum (Z4–9)
58–61
sunflower see Helianthus
annuus
Swiss chard 43, 79
Syringa (Z3–9) 84

T
Tagetes (annual) 42
T. Bonanza Series (annual) 21
T. 'Vanilla' (annual) 21
Tanacetum parthenium (Z4–9)
66–9
T. p. 'Aureum' (Z4–9) 87
T. vulgare (Z3–9) 26–9, 83
Tellima grandiflora (Z4–8)
58–61, 66–9
Teucrium (Z5–9) 42
Thymus (thyme) (Z4–9) 46, 79,
87
tomatoes 79

Trifolium rubens (Z4–8)
10–13, 26–9
Trillium (Z4–9) 68
Trollius europaeus (Z3–7) 80–3

Tropaeolum majus
(nasturtium) (annual) 79
T. m. 'Alaska' (annual) 73
Tulipa (tulips) (Z5–8) 33,
80–3, 101
T. 'Maureen' (Z6) 17
T. 'Queen of Night' (Z6)
14–17
Typha latifolia (Z3) 50–3

V
Vancouveria chrysantha (Z7)
68
Verbascum (mullein) (Z5–9) 9
V. bombyciferum (Z6) 13
V. olympicum (Z6) 30–3
Verbena 'Blue Lagoon' (Z9)
40–3
V. bonariensis (Z7–10) 54–7
V. 'Showtime' (Z9) 14–17
Veronica longifolia (Z4–8) 13,
33
V. 'Shirley Blue' (Z4–8) 13,
26–9, 33, 62–5
V. spicata subsp. incana
(Z4–8) 25
Viburnum (Z4–9) 84
Vinca minor (Z4) 68
Viola (pansies) (Z4–9) 36–9,
42, 72
V. 'Ardross Gem' (Z7) 21
V. cornuta (Z7) 26–9, 80–3
V. c. 'Victoria Cawthorne'
(Z7) 21
V. 'Huntercombe Purple'
(Z7) 21
V. odorata (heartsease)
(Z5–8) 68, 79, 84
V. pedata (Z3–8) 21
V. × wittrockiana (Z6) 80–3

YZ
Yucca filamentosa 'Ivory'
(Z5–10) 57
Y. flaccida (Z8) 57
Y. gloriosa 'Variegata'
(Z7–11) 57
zucchini 43, 79

general index

A
amendments, soil 97
annuals:
  mixed borders 28
  planting 97
  sowing 100, *100*
  two-color borders 32
autumn care 99

B
bark:
  mulches 97, 98
  paths *60*
bog gardens *48*
bricks:
  parterres *43*
  paths 83
  raised flower beds *90–91*
bronze foliage 25
bulbs:
  mixed borders 26
  planting 101, *101*
  woodland borders 60
buying plants 101

C
carpet beds *18–21*
circular beds 34, 35, *36–9*
climbing plants:
  obelisks 73
  pergolas 79
  rose trellis walk *92–5*
colors:
  foliage 25
  perennial borders 13
  purple and yellow borders *30–3*
  single-color borders *14–17*
compost 97, 99
corner planting *44–7*
cottage gardens *80–3*

D
deadheading 99
digging 96, *96*
double-digging 96, *96*
drainage, raised beds 90

drought-tolerant plants *54–7*
dry borders *49*, *54–7*
  Mediterranean borders *62–5*
  shady borders 68

E
edgings, paths 56, 60
edible borders *76–9*

F
farmyard manure 97, 99
fertilizers 97
flowers, edible borders *76–9*
focal points, round beds 38
foliage 9
  bronze 25
  foliage beds *22–5*
  gold 25
  purple 25
  silver 25
  single-color borders 16
  variegated 16, 25
foundations, raised flower beds 90
frost protection 99

G
gold foliage 25
grass paths 83
grass cuttings, mulches 98
gravel:
  gravel beds *49*
  mulches 98
  paths 56
ground-cover plants 44

H
hedges:
  parterres 40
  shaped borders *34–5*
herbs, parterres 43

I
inorganic mulches 98
island beds 12

L
leaf mold 60, 97, 98
leaves *see* foliage
liners, ponds 52
logs, bark paths *60*

M
maintenance 98
manure 97, 99
Mediterranean borders *62–5*
mixed borders *26–9*
mulches 98, 99
mushroom compost 97, 98

N
netting supports 98
north walls 69
nurseries, buying plants 101

O
obelisks 73
organic matter 96
organic mulches 98, 99
oval beds 38

P
parterres 35, *40–3*
paths:
  bark chippings 60
  cottage gardens *80–3*
  dry borders 56
  rose trellis walk *92–5*
  scented paths *84–7*
  walk-through borders *74–5*
paved areas, corner beds 46
pea stick supports 98
peat 97
perennial borders *10–13*
perennials:
  autumn care 99
  deadheading 99
  planting 97
  sowing 100, *100*
  staking 99
pergolas 79
planning 97

plant associations, roses 72
planting 97–8
  bulbs 60, 101, *101*
  carpet beds *18–21*
  roses 72
  round beds 38
  scented paths 86
  waterside borders 52
plastic mulches 98
ponds *50–3*
pruning 99–100, *99*
  lavender 86
purple and yellow borders 30–3
purple foliage 25

R
railroad ties, raised flower beds 90, *91*
raised flower beds 88–91
rock gardens 47
rope, rose trellis walk 95
round beds 34, 35, 36–9

S
safety, constructing rock gardens 47
scented paths 84–7
seasonal interest, single-color beds 17
seaweed 97
seed:
  collecting 65
  sowing 100–1, *100–1*
seedlings, pricking out 101, *101*
shady borders *48*, 66–9
  woodland borders *48*, 60
shaped borders 34–47
shrubs:

mixed borders 26–9
  planting 97, 98
  pruning 99–100, *99*
  staking 99
  two-color borders 32
  woodland borders 60
silver borders 25
single-color borders *14–17*, 35
soil:
  conditioners 97
  mulches 98
  preparation 96, *96*
sowing seed 100–1, *100–1*
special borders 48–73
spring:
  two-color borders 33
  woodland borders *61*
stakes 98, *98*, 99, *99*
standards, staking 99
stepping stones 75, *83*
stone, raised flower beds *91*
straw mulches 98
stream beds, dry *65*
string supports 99
succulents *49*, *57*
supports 98–9

T
ties, staking 99
top-dressing 99
traditional borders 8–33
training:
  obelisks 73
  shrub roses 28
trees:

planting 98
  pruning 99–100
  shady borders 68
  staking 99, *99*
  woodland borders 58–61
trellis, rose walks 92–5
twiggy-branch supports 98
two-color borders 30–3

U
underplanting:
  perennial borders 13
  rose trellis walk 94
  woodland borders *61*

V
variegated foliage 16, 25
vegetables:
  edible borders 76–9
  parterres 43

W
walk-through borders 74–95
walls, shady borders 69
watering 99
waterside planting *48*, *50–3*
weedkillers 96
weeds 96, 98, 99
wheels, round beds 39
white borders 17, *95*
wind, shady borders 68
woodland borders *48*, 58–61

Y
yellow and purple borders 30–3

credits

The publishers would like to thank the following illustrators for their contributions to the book: Elizabeth Pepperell, Martine Collings, Tracy Fennell, Valerie Hill, Stephen Hird, Sarah Kensington, Amanda Patton, Lizzie Sanders, Helen Smythe, and Ann Winterbotham.

They would also like to thank the owners of the following gardens for their help: Axletree Garden and Nursery, Peasmarsh, East Sussex; Bates Green, Arlington, East Sussex; Beth Chatto Gardens, Elmstead Market, Essex; Hailsham Grange, Hailsham, East Sussex; King John's Lodge, Etchingham, East Sussex; Merriments Garden, Hurst Green, East Sussex; Queen Anne's, Goudhurst, Kent; Rogers Rough, Kilndown, Kent; Upper Mill Cottage, Lodse, Kent; Hadspen Garden and Nursery, Castle Cary, Somerset; Cinque Cottage, Ticehurst, East Sussex; Sticky Wicket Garden, Buckland Newton, Dorset; Snape Cottage, Chaffeymoor, Dorset; Grace Barrand Design Centre, Nutfield, Surrey; Holkham Hall Garden Centre, Holkham, Norfolk; Wyland Wood, Robertsbridge, East Sussex; Long Barn, Kent; and Hatfield House, Hertfordshire.

The photographs in this book were taken by Stephen Robson except for the following which are courtesy of Jerry Harpur: (t = top, b = bottom, c = center, l = left, r = right) p.34 tr, bl, cr, br; p.35 br; p.74 tl; p.75 tl, tr, br; p.104; p.111.

acknowledgments

The author would like to thank all those involved in bringing this book
into the light of day: Anne Ryland, who made the book possible by
commissioning it; Lynn Bryan, for editorial work during the early stages,
and Sarah Polden, who took over and shaped the book into its final
form, as well as giving plenty of encouragement; Stephen Robson,
who manipulated the camera so adroitly; Mark Latter, for the hours
he spent on the design and his endless stream of faxes; and all the
illustrators for the delightful artwork.

Thanks also to all the owners of the beautiful gardens who allowed us to
photograph them especially for this book.